Freedom from

Freedom from

Evelyn Kliewer

Illustrations by Al Hartley

SPIRE BOOKS

Fleming H. Revell Company
Old Tappan, New Jersey

Library of Congress Cataloging in Publication Data

Kliewer, Evelyn.
    Freedom from fat.

    Bibliography: p.
    1. Reducing—Moral and religious aspects.
2. Reducing—Biography.   3. Reducing diets.
4. Kliewer, Evelyn.   I.   Title.
RM222.2.L5727   248'.4   77-8492
ISBN 0-8007-8308-5

This is an original Spire book, published by Spire Books,
a Division of Fleming H. Revell Company.
Old Tappan, New Jersey

To Kermit, Wendy, Bonnie, Bruce and Scott—
My family's so glad I'm no longer going to pot;
Karen Wojahn and Sheila Cragg edited this book,
And they're happy with how I'm beginning to
    look!
Ruth Walker loaned me her electric typewriter,
Which sure made the script work a whole lot
    lighter;
Speaking of lighter, let's all agree
When you finish this book, that's how you will
    be!

Contents

Introduction

Thirty-seven years ago (I was six), my mom dropped me off at the Saturday matinee. What she didn't know was that I had stolen thirty-five cents from her purse, so intense was my craving for sweets. I bought seven packages of licorice at the show, and what I hadn't consumed during the two-hour movie, I hid under my pillow at home. A lifelong pattern of compulsive eating, guilt, shame, self-pity, and self-condemnation began. Then I found the answer to my problem, two keys which unlocked the door to my freedom from fat.

If you are a compulsive eater or simply a person who eats too much, you can be delivered from your habit. This book will tell you how. Most of our considerations are heavy (pardon the pun), so we will have some fun at the end of each chapter with a bit of *"Weighty Wisdom."* Maybe you will come up with some of your own ditties and share them with me.

Happy slimming!

EVELYN KLIEWER

1

Your Weight:
Problem or Project?

Overweight is a problem to more than a hundred million Americans, says David Reuben in his book *The Save Your Life Diet*. At least it's a problem to the sixty million of them who, according to a CBS newscast of 1976, are on a diet. What a shame that only 10 percent will be successful after struggling and straining to slice off a few pounds: Dr. Reuben figures that "over 90 percent of those who lose weight gain back every pound"!

You can be one of the elite, one of the one in ten who enjoys success. But first, let's get failure out of the way.

A recent magazine article states that some people should not diet, because they get caught in a bind: obsession with wanting to lose, the inability to do it successfully. All they do is stay fat and end up frustrated.

Most of us can identify with such failure, hav-

ing taken many rides on the diet merry-go-round,
our weight Yo-Yoing up and down to the music of
each new scheme we try. And most of us are
prone to try them all.

Lisa, an attractive matron with graying hair, is
one who experiments. She read about a new
technique called Staplepuncture. One day she
stuffed her bulky frame into her station wagon,
struggled with the seat belt, and then drove the
twenty-five miles from our desert town to
Mexico. There she had staples stuck into both
ears. This treatment supposedly allows a person
to stave off appetite, although some call it pure
hokum.

Anyway, Lisa believed it—and every time she
felt the hunger pangs, she pulled her earlobes.
She developed a nagging earache, but she lost
weight. Then a sad day came: time to remove the
staples. Alas, when Lisa's crutch was removed,
her frame rapidly became bulky again.

Maria, my Spanish friend, took daily hormone
shots at six dollars per plunge and suffered on
500 calories at the same time. Both her belly and
her bottom became raw. To top it off, when she
finished that torture, she drove 300 miles round
trip, twice a week, for electric-shock treatments.
She took in the food plaguing her and she was
wired up for the kill. On taco day, she brought in
a dozen and her subconscious supposedly was
shocked into no longer salivating at such Mexi-

can goodies. Now she eats burritos and en-
chiladas instead. Lots of them.

I have not met anyone yet who has tried the
Nibble diet, recently published in a national
magazine, or the S diet (cut your S's in half:
sweets, slipperies, starches, sodas, snacks,
spirits, seconds, and salts), or the wired-jaw bit.
But I'll bet you a calorie we are all familiar with
grapefruit, hard-boiled eggs, and prunes.

Yesterday I picked up two of the leading
women's magazines prominently displayed in
every supermarket. This month you can opt for
"Eating Is Okay!" and learn how, *or* you may
choose "Eating Is *Not* Okay!" and study that one.
Both are written by medical experts.

Most of us have been exposed to the gruesome
facts about what excess weight does to our
bodies, so we will skip the gory details here
about heart attacks, diabetes, accidents, and the
rest. I wonder if knowing these facts is the
motivating stimulus, anyway, which causes us to
want to reduce. Personally, I've always found
looking honestly into my mirror pretty awful.
When I got thoroughly disgusted with what I
saw, I'd be ready to diet.

Oh, I achieved temporary success—probably
about a thousand times. Any of us can if we are
strongly motivated. But the permanent weight
loss, which comes only through a change of eating habits, seemed to elude me. I fell into the 90

percent category of those who have never been able to resist, for very long, the temptations constantly flaunted before us via TV, colorful magazine ads, grocery displays, and by family and friends. We simply do not have that kind of willpower, that confidence in our own strength.

Now, you may be a rare one whose overeating causes you no pain or interference in enjoying life. How fortunate you are—I wonder if you are a case for a museum! Most of us find we are obsessed with our problem and that it darkens every other area of our lives.

Some overweight people are so miserable they closet themselves in their homes and withdraw from the world. Others try to mask their feelings of frustration and self-hatred beneath a smile. But a majority of us feel trapped and wonder if we will ever be free from our prison of fat.

Here is the good news: If you are willing to relinquish your Battle of the Bulge to Jesus Christ, He will win it for you. He wants every one of us to realize how utterly incapable we are and how totally dependent we are upon Him to solve our problems.

He tells us: "The Spirit of the Lord God is upon me; because the Lord hath anointed me . . . to proclaim liberty to the captives, and the opening of the prison to them that are bound" (Isaiah 61:1, *see also* Luke 4:18 KJV).

God wants to establish a warm, intimate, per-

sonal relationship with each one of us. He longs
for us to present our lives to Jesus Christ, who
gives us the right to become children of God
when we receive Him. All we need to do is trust
Him to save us. (*See* John 1:12.) But *salvation*
means more than accepting Christ as Savior. As
noted in the *Handy Dictionary of the Bible* (Mer-
rill C. Tenney, editor): "Theologically, it [*salvation*] denotes . . . the whole process by which
man is delivered from all that interferes with the
enjoyment of God's highest blessings."

But God will not set us free until we *want* to be
free and until we ask Him to release us from our
bondage.

Maybe you wonder right now if you are truly a
compulsive eater. Let's use the Overeaters
Anonymous guidelines (reprinted here with
permission) and quiz ourselves:

1 Do you eat when you're not hungry?
2 Do you go on eating binges for no appar-
   ent reason?
3 Do you have feelings of guilt and remorse
   after overeating?
4 Do you give too much time and thought to
   food?
5 Do you look forward with pleasure and an-
   ticipation to the moments when you can
   eat alone?

6 Do you plan these secret binges ahead of time?

7 Do you eat sensibly before others and make up for it alone?

8 Is your weight affecting the way you live your life?

9 Have you tried to diet for a week (or longer), only to fall short of your goal?

10 Do you resent the advice of others who tell you to "use a little willpower" to stop overeating?

11 Despite evidence to the contrary, have you continued to assert that you can diet "on your own" whenever you wish?

12 Do you crave to eat at a definite time, day or night, other than mealtime?

13 Do you eat to escape from worries or trouble?

14 Has your physician ever treated you for overweight?

15 Does your food obsession make you or others unhappy?

If you answered yes to three or more of these questions, it is probable that you have a compulsive eating problem.

If we are going to continue to blame our mothers or glands or hormones or thyroid or big bones for our problem (I've done it all), and if we refuse to take the responsibility for our own overeating, God can't do much with us. We must be ruthlessly honest with ourselves. The more transparent and vulnerable we allow ourselves to become, the more quickly Jesus can work with us.

I'm thinking of a case I recently read in "Dear Abby." A woman wrote complaining that her husband is always bringing home nuts, candy, gooey pastry, and the like, then making nasty remarks about how fat *she* is. (Wouldn't you like to hear his side of the story?)

She states: "He's lucky. He can eat anything and not gain an ounce. If I just *look* at a piece of candy, I gain a pound." She was infuriated with her spouse for his thoughtlessness, and for her own lack of willpower.

Here is the tale of a woman who perhaps is not honest with herself, for none of us gains a pound from *looking* at anything. I suspect the communication in this marriage is poor, which could be partly due to lack of openness with one another. But I also suspect the woman blames her husband for *her* own overeating, and I wonder if she is really desperate enough to face her problem realistically.

Jesus does not want you bound to food (or anything else). He doesn't want you to have a problem; He wants you to be His project. He wants to teach you to relax, to learn to give your burdens to Him and just bask in His peace. One of the greatest blessings you will find as a Christian is taking advantage of the strength of the Lord instead of trying to do things your way, in your own power.

God adores having you as His personal project. He created the universe and He created *you*. He is personal and practical. He pours out His love on a one-to-one basis.

God loves you so personally that He knows every detail about you: your inner needs, your body chemistry, your compulsions. He will reveal to you why you eat, be it psychological, bad habits, biochemical sensitivities, or whatever. God will show you the root causes of your overweight and heal them. He will teach you what to do about your problem, devising a custom-made plan, a perfect one, specifically for your individual weight-control program.

God promises success when He is in control. Success may follow a process of pruning, inner healing, refining and disciplining, or deliverance. God does not always give us the "Promised Land" or victorious life all at once. But when we are free, we are free indeed.

The premises set forth in this book all rest upon your personal relationship with God, through Jesus Christ.

If you have never accepted Jesus as your personal Savior, He now waits to offer you love and forgiveness. "Behold, I stand at the door, and knock: if any man hear my voice, and open the door, I will come in to him . . ." (Revelation 3:20 KJV).

God's Word states that we have all sinned (Romans 3:23) and that we are therefore separated from fellowship with Him. He restores us to Himself through Jesus. "If we confess our sins, he is faithful and just to forgive us our sins, and to cleanse us from all unrighteousness" (1 John 1:9 KJV). God makes no other provision for our salvation. "I am the Way—yes, and the Truth and the Life. No one can get to the Father except by means of Me" (John 14:6).

Here is a prayer you may pray now to receive Christ:

Dear Jesus, I want to receive You as my personal Savior and Lord of my life. Thank You that You died for my sins and thank You for forgiving me and cleansing me. I now submit my life to You. Amen.

According to Scripture which we have stated, if you have prayed this prayer Christ has come to reside within you, and you now have eternal life. Your sins have been forgiven and you are a child of God.

Next, let's pray together about our weight problems:

Heavenly Father, I thank You that You love me so personally and care about every detail of my life. I now relinquish to You this problem of overeating and ask You to take charge of this part of my life, too. Teach me about You and about myself. Teach me to listen to Your voice directing me. I ask You to release me from this bondage of food. I will obey what You tell me to do. In Jesus' name. Amen.

CATALYST

I passed a mirror. It's plain to see. There is far
too much of me! (Apparently, I've overdone, but
eating has been so much fun.)

To wear fashion with a flare,
I am now aware . . .
I must pare . . .
The spare.

2

You've Come
a Long Way, Baby!

I waited far too long before allowing God to conquer my compulsive cravings, correct my eating habits, and turn them into His way of life. It was thirty-seven years after the addiction started that I became a recovered foodaholic. It is my hope that you will receive enough help from this book that you will trust God to set you free from this problem. First, I want to give you some idea of what a mess I was.

For years I hid sweets under my pillow, helpless to gain control over my eating. So conscious of my weight problem was I that in sixth grade I entered and won a contest sponsored by our metropolitan newspaper. My certificate of merit for writing a winning "Fat Boy" dittie (I've long since forgotten what I wrote) is included at the end of this chapter.

By college, I shot up to 175 pounds, stuffing my five-foot-four frame into a size 18 or 20 dress.

Once I was shopping (probably for sweets) at a quaint little grocery near campus, the kind with tiny aisles and floors that are uneven and go up and down.

As I pushed my cart along, cans began falling down from the shelves. I turned crimson and thought, *I am so fat that just pushing my grocery cart down this asle is causing vibrations. What will I do?* As fast as I tried to restack the cans, they fell again.

Embarrassed, I went to the owner and said, "I'm so sorry. I've knocked cans off your shelves, but they won't stay back up."

He laughed at my profuse apology and replied, "Didn't you know? We just had a little earthquake."

That incident motivated me to head for our college psychiatric clinic for the emotionally disturbed. The psychiatrist used the technique of staring at me, hoping I suppose, that I would break down and divulge secrets from the deep recesses of my subconscious, so she could analyze me. I wanted to cry my heart out and feel someone cared, but I could not. So we just stared at each other for half an hour each week while I grew fatter. My grades plummeted and I lost my scholarship for the next year.

Our college also had a medical clinic, which I tried. "Let's put you on a low-calorie diet," the doctor suggested. I faithfully followed the program for six months, but only by chewing twelve packages of candy-coated gum each day. I bought it by the case and hid it under my bed.

By that summer twenty pounds were shed, and then a friend and I went job hunting.

Ann said, "I'm so hot and tired and hungry. Let's stop for an ice cream."

I hesitated, but I hadn't tasted anything interesting for half a year and it sounded good. One lick and I went berserk. The craving for sweets returned, and by fall term I looked like a ball of blubber again.

After graduating from the university I met my husband-to-be, who fortunately saw something worthwhile behind the fat and married me anyway. I squeezed my then 155 pounds (I starved off 20 after meeting Kermit) into a borrowed wedding gown. Even now, I am reluctant to view our wedding pictures.

In college I had discovered coffee and cigarettes (from which Jesus later delivered me). Soon after marriage, Kermit and I found a doctor who specialized in weight control through amphetamines and hormones—all colors and sizes and at an enormous fee.

He weighed me and said, "Here are your pills for two weeks. I'll see you again then for a refill. Don't eat any fat, but you can have all the sugar you want." He offered us a plate of orange gumdrops to prove his point.

For six weeks, sleep eluded me as I sat up and chain-smoked and coughed and drank coffee. But I lost weight rapidly, which was obvious to anyone who saw my gaunt, drawn face on which was just as rapidly appearing a mustache and a beard.

The next try for help was when I joined a weight club. One evening I had the misfortune of gaining half a pound, the highest gain of the night, so I was asked to come up front (while everyone giggled) and sing the "I'm a Pig" song. I was then handed a huge pair of "pig" pants, with firm instructions to display them for all the world to see. Humiliated, I drowned my sorrow in a hot-fudge sundae, tore up the britches and never returned to the group.

Some of my erratic eating made me feel kooky. There were chocolate-coated ice-cream bars in the bathtub and frozen pies and cookies in the garage, most of which tasted simply awful.

One Halloween I gleefully hit all the stores, happy for an excuse to load up on trick-or-treat goodies, and promptly hid them in my cedar chest for later consumption—by me.

Night eating was the worst. The procedure was to get up, grope to the fridge in a semi-stupor, butter several slices of bread, and meander back to bed to eat them. One morning I reached around and found a piece of squashed buttered bread firmly attached to my derrière. Coming to my senses, I cried out, "My God, what have I done?"

Whenever I could wake myself up enough to become rational, I would fight eating for hours. One November, all our Christmas cards found themselves addressed during a night spent fighting to stay away from food. But usually there was only a strange, detached awareness of what I was doing.

The only way to stick to any sort of program was to chew gum, tons of it, stuffing in one piece after another until I was up to 100 pieces of bubble gum or 25 packs of stick gum every night. I kept chewing even after all my upper teeth were gone. Every time I tried to quit, I'd climb the walls.

By sharing this with you (and it hasn't been easy), I hope no one will feel that he or she's any stranger or has more of a problem than I did. I was a total mess—and if God delivered me, He most certainly can deliver you!

A couple of years after I became a Christian, I offered this prayer to God: "Lord, why do I have such a problem? I want to yield and submit to You, yet there is something wrong. You've helped me in so many areas of my life, why not here? I can't do it on my own. Teach me what to do."

My prayer seemed to go unanswered. I kept a ledger for three years thereafter and ran a recur-

ring story. Success one day, failure the next.
Mostly failure. A theme of self-disgust at my inability to cope with my weight problem per-
meated my whole life until I was totally obsessed
with the problem.

Friends prayed for me upon request, or I'd
raise my hand for "unspoken prayer" at church.
This seemed to strengthen me for a few days;
then I'd go berserk again. One day I even shook
my fist at God and shouted, "Don't You even
care?"

I wondered how God could think very much of
me when I was so weak and helpless. Little did I
realize that when we are in that humble position,
God finally has something to work with.

I felt terribly self-conscious and remember one
miserable day in particular. Kermit and the boys
and I were camping in our tent on a piece of
property where we are developing avocados. I
arranged to meet a group of ladies and go with
them to a Christian seminar. I had thrown a dress
into my suitcase, and when I put it on in the tent,
I realized too late that I had made a mistake in
my choice.

At the meeting, a friend, Dee, ran up to me and
blurted, "Evelyn! Are you pregnant?" Another
(someone I had not seen in several years) hugged
me and shouted for all the world to hear, "Why,
you little fattie!" Tears stung my eyes and my
cheeks flushed.

At the seminar, I listened to several teachings, one on fasting. Uncomfortable, I squirmed throughout the presentation. Something within me seemed to be fighting the whole message. I approached the speaker afterward and talked with her. I told her, "Ever since I have been a Christian, my problem with weight has accelerated. I have tried listening to sermons, prayer, reading books and Scripture, but nothing does any good. I am a helpless foodaholic and don't know where to turn."

She suggested I pray "Lord, show me by Your Spirit how to pray for my body to be delivered from this driving obsession."

I did, and finally—thirteen months later—I was free.

ELMER'S
"NO-BELLY"
PRIZE

Certifying beyond the shadow of a calorie that:

Evelyn Durland

*is a member of the Fat Boy's SPACE CONTROL, having
written a non-caloric dittie which appeared in
newspapers throughout the United States
and in most foreign countries.*

Elmer "Sizzle" Wheeler
Head Ex-Fat Boy

3

Freedom

The first step to my freedom came after God revealed to me what I should have suspected years earlier: a food sensitivity. My initial clue came when I discovered gum is loaded with corn sugar. Every time I ate anything else containing corn sugar, I wanted more—and more and more and more, ad infinitum. Yet I tried cutting it out and still had problems. Every morning I'd vow to be good; by evening I'd be a bloated bilious mess.

I feel this problem of food addiction is far more common than most people realize. It is a big revelation to find out that one is not necessarily a psychological case. The problem may be entirely caused by a food intolerance, although poor eating habits may have developed over the years as a result of not knowing what foods to avoid biochemically. Many years of compulsive eating, even if due to a food addiction, are bound to have caused secondary psychological problems which must now be conquered.

Through sleuthing and a book sent my way, God revealed to me that my body can handle neither refined sugars nor starches. They both trigger off compulsive eating, and I react just as an alcoholic reacts to alcohol.

Healings do not always happen overnight. I had to wait patiently for God to answer my prayer. In the intervening months, I felt rather hopeless.

My healing came in two phases: through God's *revelation* to me that my body cannot tolerate certain foods, and through *obedience to* that revelation from God. The empowerment for obedience comes through Him and cannot be mustered up on our own. I have been set free from my flesh, free to abstain from the wrong foods for me and from the necessity and compulsion to have them. My eating is now controlled by walking in the Spirit and resisting temptation.

Regardless of the cause of your compulsive eating or overweight problem, God will give you a personalized success formula. But you must be willing to listen to Him and to obey what He tells you to do. And listening to the voice of the Holy Spirit, at least for me, is a learning process, often a long and painful one. Willingness to listen wins half the battle. "In everything you do, put God first, and he will direct you and crown your efforts with success" (Proverbs 3:6).

THE SYNDROME

I'm ashamed to admit it,
But I sneak sustenance at night,
Even though my daytime food's
An epicure's delight.
I'm sure it's my subconscious
Which is feeling quite deprived.
To outwit that subliminal self,
Here's the scheme which I've contrived:

> A gate across the doorway, a chair in front of
> that,
> The cookie jar is set up high to help combat
> the fat.

When I next go groping in the dark obscurity,
For some delightful nutriment to set subconscious free,
I'll not, I trust, get very far. The battlefield is set.

> I'll trip and fumble back to bed.
> I'll be the loser yet!

4

Receive Yourself

One winter night is still vivid to me. We lived in Palmdale, California, where my husband was teaching. I couldn't sleep and got up to peek out the window.

"Kermit," I called excitedly, "come see. It's snowing!" I had never seen it snow and watched, fascinated. My practical spouse thought I was crazy because I sat up all night, transfixed. I thought about how each tiny snowflake is unique, an individual creation of God. How like that we are! God's creations, each of us fashioned by His hand. Imagine how boring life would be if we all looked exactly the same (size 10 for the ladies; 32 waist for the men) with identical personalities and talents.

Yet, so many of us do not feel at all good about ourselves. I understand that as high a percentage as nine out of ten of us put ourselves down.

A big part of being free is learning to accept ourselves, and we don't have to wait until we look perfect on the outside. Nevertheless, personal appearance is one of the greatest drawbacks people feel they suffer, according to a recent study by Bill Gothard's Institute in Basic Youth Conflicts. Most overweight people, in fact, cross their bodies off as *yuk*. Sometimes subconsciously, but *yuk* nonetheless. When we look at our outside and dislike it, it affects our inner feelings, too. And how we feel about ourselves colors all of our relationships in life, even our feelings about God. We are so accustomed to putting ourselves down, we expect Him to condemn us, too.

Yet God tells us that He created us in His image and that His creation is *good*. Does God lie? "Woe to the man who fights with his Creator. Does the pot argue with its maker? Does the clay dispute with him who forms it, saying, 'Stop, you're doing it wrong!' or the pot exclaim, 'How clumsy can you be!'? Woe to the baby just being born who squalls to his father and mother, 'Why have you produced me? Can't you do anything right at all?' " (Isaiah 45:9, 10).

We are not to question the work of God's hands (us) but rather to accept ourselves and yield any imperfections to Him. Let Him be concerned with your appearance, while you bask in His peace. I recommend that you study the entire 139th Psalm. A friend, Sally, did just that. She

had been through a divorce and felt totally un-
worthy and unloved. Psalm 139 ministered a
life-change to her as she realized the fact that
God loves her—Sally—and cares for the tiniest
detail of her life.

God knows where we stand and where we fall.
He knows our thoughts, even when they are
deep within us. He protects and keeps us, and we
cannot surprise God. All these facts are stated in
the first few verses of the psalm.

We see that we cannot hide from God. He
wanted us and made us and did not make any
mistake in creating us. We are to praise Him. God
didn't just plop you together, He *worked* at it.
Let that sink deep within you and minister to
you:

> You made all the delicate, inner parts of
> my body, and knit them together in my
> mother's womb. Thank you for making me so
> wonderfully complex! It is amazing to think
> about. Your workmanship is marvelous—and
> how well I know it. You were there while I
> was being formed in utter seclusion! You
> saw me before I was born and scheduled
> each day of my life before I began to breathe.
> Every day was recorded in your Book! How
> precious it is, Lord, to realize that you are
> thinking about me constantly! I can't even

count how many times a day your thoughts
turn towards me. And when I waken in the
morning, you are still thinking of me!

Psalms 139:13–18

God planned you as a unique individual—food
intolerances included! Now, it is true that God
looks inside us. ". . . for the Lord sees not as
man sees; man looks on the outward appearance,
but the Lord looks on the heart" (1 Samuel 16:7
RSV). So you may wonder why it is important to
God to help us with our overweight problems.

God wants us to be happy. And He knows full
well that it is very hard to be happy and con-
tented and full of joy on the inside if we don't
like our outer shell. And what do we, and others,
look at? Our outsides! John E. Gibson's "People
Quiz" in *Family Weekly* asks, "How much does
appearance really count?" and shows that most
people judge us by the way we look. Happily,
studies at Ohio State University also show that
our facial expressions clearly dominate the per-
ception of liking or disliking.

A radiant Christian countenance is certainly
more important than our figure, and God doesn't
want us all hung up on "thin is in." But He does
want us aware that sloppy fat, hanging all over
the place (or even well girdled) is not a good
Christian witness and is not healthy. My friend

Pat puts it succinctly: "How can God find room to live in me when there's so much fat down there crowding Him out?"

If looking at ourselves in the mirror causes self-consciousness or self-rejection, that is a big concern of our Heavenly Father. He wants us to be able to look in that mirror and smile! Jesus deals with our whole person, inner and outer, not just a fragmented part of us.

The reason God created us is to express Himself through us. Our talents and abilities are unique and we need to find out what God put inside each of us, so that all that is locked within can be let out. God wants us yielded to Him so that He can flow through us, expressing and developing our hidden potential.

One of your joys as a Christian should be to find new expressions for your creativity. As you learn to receive yourself—to find yourself—in Jesus, you will also learn to put aside the importance of food and find satisfaction through walking in the Spirit, allowing God's creativity to flow through you.

As a youngster, I studied piano, then tired of it and quit. About twenty-five years later I received Christ into my life and became active in a church. Someone was needed to accompany the choir. Shyly, I said, "I'll try." And it has been very rewarding. The only damper ever put on the enjoyment of this expression was when one of the dear church ladies suggested I wear a one-piece undergarment to firm me up.

I found a creative flow coming into my writing, too, and have felt great satisfaction (and a lot of frustration) in this ministry. It is hard work, but fulfilling.

Other friends have discovered talent in working with children, in cake decorating, in handcrafts, and in visiting the elderly or sick.

My friend Kay prayed about how God would wish to use her in His service. As a result, she has started the first Sunday-school class for mentally retarded adults in our community.

Phil, another friend, has developed a leatherworking talent into a business operation. The beauty of his hand tooling and design blesses many.

Lucille has learned she has a beautiful teaching ministry, and she brings the Word of God to an interdenominational group of women each week, besides teaching a mixed Sunday-school class at her church. Lives are being changed because of her commitment.

Others work quietly behind the scenes. One friend, Selma, is the gal who *always* remembers everyone's birthday, anniversary, and all those special occasions with a lovely card. My children look forward to her valentines on February 14, her cards on their birthdays, and her Christmas goodies. Many people appreciate her thoughtfulness.

I'm sure you could think of as many examples. Ask God to reveal to you what is down inside and to help you bring it to the surface, to be used for Him.

Finally, we need to realize that we are worth so much individually to God that he sent His only Son, Jesus, to pay the price for our sins and to restore us into fellowship with Him. Continue to yield yourself to Him, and ask Him to use you, your talents and abilities, for His glory.

This is a good time for us to have a little talk with God, so shall we pray together?

Father, thank You that I am so important to You. Thank You that You spent time thinking about me and creating me so that You could reveal Your glory through me. Help me to love and appreciate myself, just the way You created me.

Father, I thank You for any talent or ability You have given me. Help me to discover what is deep within myself, so that I may be a blessing to others. Help me to learn more about You every day. Cause Your Word to come alive in my heart. In Jesus' name. Amen.

OPPOSITES

A calorie is very wee,
An abstract I can't even see
Until I overeat.

Then it's very matter-of-fact,
The form no longer is abstract.
It's quite concrete!

5

New Beginnings

After my deliverance from compulsive eating of sugars and starches, I found a new understanding of the concept of flesh as opposed to spirit. This understanding has enriched my life and enabled me to be victorious in my fight against fat. It can mean victory for you, too.

A non-Christian is ruled by his fleshly desires, by his basic human nature. He doesn't know anything about walking in the Spirit. But if we as Christians acknowledge the lordship of Jesus Christ in our lives, we should be ruled by the Holy Spirit. "But clothe yourself with the Lord Jesus Christ, the Messiah, and make no provision for [indulging] the flesh" (Romans 13:14 AMPLIFIED).

Every time we yield to the impulses of the flesh—what *we* want—we alienate ourselves from our consciousness of the presence of God. How can we feel close to Him and full of joy when we fight what we know He wants for us?

Instead, we become full of inner turmoil, feeling anxious and pressured.

At times we may feel we are standing still and wonder how God can have one more ounce of patience with us! But His love knows no measure. We must keep totally honest before Him and continue to submit our flesh to His control *until food becomes something we eat only to live, and no longer live to eat.* There is no other route to permanent weight loss.

God, who is all power, all wisdom, and all knowledge, wants to direct every fiber of our being. I find it helps to pray this way the first thing each morning: *"Jesus, I present my body to You as a living sacrifice. Help me bring it into what is good, acceptable, and pleasing to You."* (*See* Romans 12:1, 2).

I've been reading in Exodus 16 how God gave the Israelites manna to sustain them day by day as they wandered in the wilderness. The ones who hoarded found the extra manna spoiled, and they had to gather it fresh daily. This has such a spiritual application—we must renew our spiritual strength on a day-to-day basis—but I also wonder: Why did they hoard? They must have felt insecure, afraid of not having enough to eat. I think compulsive eaters subconsciously do the same thing. We must learn to eat to sustain our daily needs only, trusting Jesus day by day to meet both our physical and spiritual needs.

God *always* meets His promises, for He is unchanging. If we commit our overweight problem to Him, He will take care of it. We must be patient as God brings His promises to pass. If we try to fulfill the promise for Him, we will be out of His perfect will. Then, our healing is delayed.

For example, after I had already gone to God with my problem, I jumped into a certain weight-control program. It was not the answer for me, and God tried to speak through my husband—but I didn't listen. I had no patience and I did not trust God for His answer. So I tried my own ways. I stepped out of God's perfect will.

Even so, since I had committed my problem to Him, He kept working on me. In this program of which I am speaking, I learned to cook low-calorie recipes, for which I am grateful. But I got into "doing my own thing" instead of constantly looking to God for the answers.

I had learned nothing about crucifying my own desires. Instead, I constantly concerned myself about being "legal." I thought about what I had eaten, what I was eating, and what I was about to eat. I ignored the Scripture, "Therefore, I tell you, stop being perpetually uneasy (anxious and worried) about your life, what you shall eat *or what you shall drink*, and about your body, what you shall put on. Is not life greater [in quality] than food, and the body [far above and more ex-

cellent] than clothing?" (Matthew 6:25 AMPLI-
FIED).

I did not understand the need to absolutely
crucify my fleshly desires, to lay them on God's
altar and nail them firmly down. I didn't know a
thing about my body chemistry or the need to
remain strong in God's Word. I did not understand the absolute freedom from the bondage of
the flesh which is ours through Jesus Christ.
"Therefore my people are gone into captivity,
because they have no knowledge . . ." (Isaiah
5:13 KJV).

We must be fully aware that we are in a con-
stant warfare between the Spirit and the flesh.
The one we coddle the most is going to win out.
"For we wrestle not against flesh and blood, but
against principalities, against powers, against the
rulers of the darkness of this world, against
spiritual wickedness in high places" (Ephesians
6:12 KJV).

We sometimes need to come against these
powers of darkness, which simply means taking
our rightful authority as a child of God. Jesus has
already won the battle for you on Calvary.

Arlene is a case in point. Plagued by years of
compulsive eating, she became desperate. She
would hear little voices tormenting her. One
would say, "Today I have to go to work and, oh
dear, there won't be anything for me to eat there.
Better go prepared." Another voice would

whisper, "Yippee . . . what an excuse to eat what I want!" Satan kept an inner battle raging, which totally frustrated Arlene. And sure enough, at work she ate everything in sight.

Arlene tried to "be good" but to no avail. I felt, after seeking God about her case, that she needed to stand firm against the enemy. I prayed very simply, "Satan and demon powers, I come against you and bind you in the mighty name of Jesus. I command you to leave Arlene's body alone and quit tormenting her. You have no right to harass her, as she is God's child."

Arlene has felt totally free inside since—not free of temptation, but free to choose not to give in to that temptation. She has lost several pounds in a very short time.

If you have accepted Christ, you have all power over Satan. "No one who has become part of God's family makes a practice of sinning, for Christ, God's Son, holds him securely and the devil cannot get his hands on him" (1 John 5:18). Stand up for your rights!

But don't blame Satan every time you disobey God. Many times it is ourselves, not Satan, we must deal with.

BATTLE OF THE BULGE

Her pantyhose are pinching, her girdle is too
   tight,
Her dresses snuggle closely, her skirts don't fit
   quite right.
She wonders if she'll always be destined to this
   plight?

Oh! It's the Battle of the Bulge.

Her calories are counted, her exercises done,
Her scales are tuned and ready, her cycle's on the
   run.
She hopes someday she'll reach her goal and
   have a little fun.

Oh! It's the Battle of the Bulge.

Her freezer's full of seafood, her fridge has lo-cal
   treats,
Her shelves are stocked with Shasta, her pantry
   . . . not one sweet.
She's trying hard to conquer fat and won't accept
   defeat.

Oh! It's the Battle of the Bulge.

Despite her valiant efforts in her exercising class,
Despite the low-cal menus, the periodic fasts,
She has to have her Twinkies or she swears she'll
   never last.

Oh! It's the Battle of the Bulge.

Written by Wendy Kliewer
at age 16

6

Let's Take a Walk

Walking in the Spirit is a matter of choice, just as choosing *not* to indulge the flesh is an act of the will. We are talking in terms of serving Jesus and allowing God to conform us to His image.

I find I travel fastest along the spiritual walkway when I spend time in Scripture study, prayer, and praise first thing in the morning. Beginning the day in this fashion sets my mind on God. The more I worship and praise, the fuller I feel of God, leaving less room for self and its indulgences.

"What about me?" you may ask. Perhaps you are a young mother whose family makes demands from early morning to late evening. Train yourself to catch just a few moments (you may have to use the bathroom for privacy) and say, *"Good morning, God. This is Your day and I give myself to You. Please allow me a little time alone with You later. Thank You for Your love."*

The men I know who are growing spiritually

are the ones who set aside time for God before going out into the world and its demands upon them for the day.

I used to be exhausted and slept long night hours, taking a nap as well. Since I have eliminated sugars and starches from my diet, my sleep needs have decreased rather significantly. I find myself waking quite early and it is a real joy to use this time in fellowship with the Lord. Sometimes I don't manage to get up before everyone else, and I find God is always faithful to give me some other section of the day for Him.

You may well find that as you change your eating habits, your energy level will increase and you will have more time for fellowship with God. But you *must* somehow find time for this fellowship, for the feeding from Heaven, if you want to be successful in your fight against the flesh. In fact, it was when I determined to read the Bible from cover to cover that it began to come alive to me. The release from the bondage of flesh came shortly after I began this daily discipline of study.

In order to walk in the Spirit, we need to be filled to overflowing. The Holy Spirit is the greatest appetite suppressor you can use. The fuller we are of Him, the less room there is for natural appetite. "Walk by the Spirit, and do not gratify the desires of the flesh. For the desires of the flesh are against the Spirit, and the desires of

the Spirit are against the flesh . . ." (Galatians
5:16, 17 RSV).

Do you desire to be filled with the Spirit?
Matthew 5:6 promises that if we hunger and
thirst after righteousness, we shall be filled. This
means the Spirit-empowered life. Shall we pray
together now?

*Father, I yield to You and ask You to fill
me with Your Holy Spirit. Thank You that
this is a promise to me. In Jesus' name.*

You will find that after your initial infilling of
the Holy Spirit, you will need to ask God to keep
you filled. This should be our daily prayer, that
God fill us to the brim. As we yield to the Holy
Spirit, we find a desire to go His way. A friend,
Judy, prays this way often:

*Father, I am willing to go Your way. I
don't fully understand Your ways, but I accept them as being much better than mine. I
give You permission to cause me to walk according to Your will and purpose. Make me
willing where I am unwilling to put an area
of my life under Your authority.*

Gluttony (eating to excess) is a selfish desire to
meet our own needs. I'm thinking of Andrea, a
casual acquaintance I met at a party one day.

Somehow we began speaking of eating and she confessed that she often bakes a dozen cupcakes, serves four to her family for dinner dessert and hoards the other eight. She deliberately arises in the night (I forgot to ask her if she sets her alarm) to consume them. This is gluttony.

I know the feeling, for at times when I would sit in the bathtub, soaking in pink bubbles and eating chocolate candy bars, I seemed to enjoy what I was doing. But once I was willing to listen to God's directions for my life, really listen to the Holy Spirit's leading and be obedient to His voice, healing came.

I think, in fact, it came when I became gut-level honest with God. *"Jesus,"* I prayed, *"I really am not sure if I want to be healed from this compulsive eating or not. Sometimes I think I do, deep down, and yet when I binge and know full well what I am doing, I'm not so sure. I am willing for You to make me willing to give all this to You, in Your own way and time. Do whatever needs to be done deep inside me, in my subconscious, through inner healing, to make me want to be well. I trust You. Amen."*

We need to be so superconscious of God's presence and so strong in His Word that we can face anything, even temptations to go off the eating program Jesus designs for us. "This High Priest of ours understands our weaknesses, since he had the same temptations we do, though he never once gave way to them and sinned. So let us come boldly to the very throne of God and *stay there* to receive his mercy and to find grace to help us in our times of need" (Hebrews 4:15, 16, italics added).

Another strength comes from working with other Christians as you fight life's battles. It is extremely important, I feel, that any group we get into be Christ-centered. I have one friend who was talked into going with another gal to a weight program which was costing her several dollars each week. After she began the program, she realized it was not God's answer for her, as this particular group pushes self-help and self-determination, which are contrary to God's desire that we rely on Him for strength. "Don't be teamed with those who do not love the Lord, for what do the people of God have in common with the people of sin? How can light live with darkness? And what harmony can there be between Christ and the devil? How can a Christian be a partner with one who doesn't believe?" (2 Corinthians 6:14, 15).

You might check around for Bible-study sessions in your area which relate to weight control and pray before attending them. Or perhaps you will find it works well, as I have, to have a couple of prayer partners. Selma, Pat, and I often pray via phone when we are having a special fight with fat—or just to praise God for victories. We each know we can call upon the others anytime for help. "And one standing alone can be attacked and defeated, but two can stand back-to-back and conquer; three is even better, for a triple-braided cord is not easily broken" (Ecclesiastes 4:12).

Shirley works with another friend fighting the Battle of the Bulge. They meet weekly for prayer and sharing. One of their main goals is to encourage each other to develop new eating habits according to God's leading. They discuss the psychological aspects, the problems in their childhoods and personalities which hinder their losing weight. For instance, one was stuffed by her mother as a child and food became a reward symbol. The other gal, Ruth, went days without food because of neglect and now overeats because of starvation fears.

Among the problems Shirley and Ruth pray about and discuss are:

- Shirley's temper, which goes wild when she controls her eating. She eats everyone up with her words and is seeking the Lord's control here.
- Shirley's cousin who lost 100 pounds. The husband felt so threatened and worried that

his wife would now be attractive to other
men that he made life miserable for her until
she regained every pound. The girls are in
prayer for this couple to seek the counseling
they so desperately need.

- Our new self-images as we become slim.
  Some people have been overweight most of
  their lives and take a long time to view themselves as thin once they lose weight.

- Our new attractiveness, especially to men.
  When our bodies are fat and we think of ourselves as *yuk*, we don't usually have this
  problem. In fact, some people stay fat to pro-
  tect themselves from the opposite sex. Once
  we become desirable and appealing, we
  have a responsibility not to be flirtatious or to
  encourage the attentions of the opposite sex
  if we are married.

- Our thought lives. Men may find a new problem with lust, women with fantasies. Our
  thoughts must be brought into subjection to
  the Spirit. "Now your attitudes and thoughts
  must all be constantly changing for the better. Yes, you must be a new and different
  person, holy and good. Clothe yourself with
  this new nature" (Ephesians 4:23, 24).

- Dress. We must be careful to dress modestly
  and not appear to be seductive or wear revealing clothing.

Shirley told me, "I just had a friend tell me that she was sorry to hear I was losing weight because all the women in the church would have to worry about their husbands. She meant it!"

Shirley and Ruth, however, take their responsibilities as Christian women very seriously and both are striving to lead holy and pure lives in all areas.

The more we die to self, the more alive the Spirit of God becomes within us. We find this basic principle throughout creation: death brings life. Jesus gives many illustrations, explaining that when we die, we come alive in Him and bear much fruit, like a cluster of grapes. This fruit of the Spirit is listed in Galatians 5:22, 23, and I like the way the Amplified New Testament expresses it: "But the fruit of the (Holy) Spirit, [the work which His presence within accomplishes]—is love, joy (gladness), peace, patience (an even temper, forbearance), kindness, goodness (benevolence), faithfulness; (Meekness, humility) gentleness, self-control (self-restraint, continence) . . . ."

With the Jesus System of Weight Control, the whole secret is that *He* is in control; *He* gives you the deliverance you may need; *He* provides the strength and power for you to live in the Spirit and sustain success. You rely on His strength, not your own methods. "I don't use human plans and methods to win my battles" (2 Corinthians 10:3).

Listen to God's voice and let Him talk with you about the individual program He has in mind just for you. God will see you through to victory. With Jesus, you can't lose—or should I say, All you *can* do is lose!

MOMENT OF TRUTH

Scales
Don't tell tall tales.

7

God Speaks

Acknowledging God is not mystical. It is a simple act, just as simple as opening your door to the sound of a bell. But listening is a learned skill. I find it takes time to learn to listen to God's voice—and I still make mistakes.

A marvelous teaching on hearing God's voice was presented in September 1974, at a Southern California Women's Retreat. Joy Dawson ministered, and with her permission I want briefly to discuss some of her points, intermingled with my own thoughts. (I highly recommend your ordering her tapes, listed with the address in the bibliographical section at the close of this book.)

First, we need to understand who God is, His character. Just as we seek to understand our family and friends by studying them, we must study God as revealed in Scripture if we are to know Him in a vital relationship.

God is all knowledge, all power, all wisdom, and much more. Therefore, He has answers to everything we will ever need to know, and the ability to communicate those answers to us. Study Proverbs 2 for more understanding of this concept.

God will give us detailed instructions for anything in our lives we need to know. God can and will teach you how to eat to benefit your body, which He created and knows intimately. "I will instruct thee and teach thee in the way which thou shalt go: I will guide thee with mine eye" (Psalms 32:8, 9 KJV).

We must train ourselves to go to God when we have a problem, expecting Him to answer in His own way and in His own time. It is important to test these answers, because sometimes we try to arrange circumstances or manipulate people in order to do what *we want* to do. It is true that God will frequently open or close doors and arrange circumstances, but circumstances must always line up with God's Word and be accompanied by inner peace. God never directs us against His written Word. His will for us is *never* in conflict with the Bible.

We must will to die to both our human reason and our human desire if we want our ears open to God's instructions: "Trust in the Lord with all thine heart; and lean not unto thine own understanding. In all thy ways acknowledge him, and he shall direct thy paths" (Proverbs 3:5, 6 KJV).

We hear three voices: self, Satan, and God. Self speaks to us through the avenues of human reason

and human desire. Joy Dawson suggests
this sort of prayer: "*God, with my whole will, I
die at this point to all human reasoning. It
doesn't matter what I think at all. All that mat-
ters is what You know to be the truth.*"

Likewise, we must put aside what we feel,
what we want to do, what we don't want to do.
We have already talked about learning to walk in
the Spirit. I may feel like eating all day long
(praise God, I usually don't anymore, but you
might), or I might want to go on a total fast for
days, trying to thin down in a rush, or I might
want to eat sugar or flour products. That can be
my human desire standing in God's way. When
we pray a prayer relinquishing all our human desires to God, we have taken a giant step onto the
walkway of the Spirit.

There is also another force that we battle
against, the force of Satan and his demons. They
can make suggestions to our minds; therefore we
need to silence them. Joy Dawson suggests we
silence them by this type of prayer, which must
be said firmly and with absolute faith in God's
Word and the power in the name of the Lord
Jesus Christ: "*Satan and demon powers, I come
against you in the mighty name of the Lord Jesus
Christ. I silence you and command you not to
speak or to bring any impression to my mind. It
is written, 'Resist the devil and he will flee from
you'* (James 4:7)."

It is vital that we know this: Impressions from God are always accompanied by strong inner conviction and peace in our hearts. Although God speaks in many ways, as outlined in Mrs. Dawson's tape on that subject, His communication with us is always accompanied by inner peace.

If you feel inner turmoil about a decision, do not act. Learn to be patient and wait for God's personalized answer to you. Ask God to teach you to visit with Him so that you get a good two-way communication going. He will be delighted, and soon you will say, "God told me . . ." or "God said I am to . . . ." And you will know it to be so, although you must use discretion when you speak these words to others. Many do not understand how God can possibly speak to an individual.

Your life will be rich when you "love God with all your heart and soul and mind and strength" (*see* Deuteronomy 6:5), when you obey His voice, and when you trust Him to meet with you.

WEIGHT REVIEW

She read her scale and
Condensed the tale.

8

Obedience

A counterpart of walking in the Spirit and hearing God speak is obedience, which to God is better than sacrifice. (*See* 1 Samuel 15:22.) Your freedom from bondage comes as you understand the *truths* in God's Word, as they become *alive* to you, and as you *act* on them.

We must be willing to stay under a continuous discipline to maintain our freedom. Only through the power of the Holy Spirit within can we be so good. I had an experience recently which was based on obedience and demonstrated vividly to me both my growth in the Spirit and the blessings God bestows upon those who obey Him.

As I prepared to attend a writers' conference at a fancy hotel, I had a talk with God. By now I was fasting at breakfast and I said, "Surely, God, You don't expect me to skip breakfast when I've already paid for it?"

He loudly answered, inside me, "Indeed I do, little one. The circumstances are not important. You know perfectly well I have ordained for you to cut out the morning meal until I instruct you differently."

"Okay, okay, Lord," I said, "but how about lunches and dinners? What will I do if there isn't anything I can eat?" I asked Him if I should take along tuna, hard-boiled eggs, and such.

"My soon-to-be-wee-one," He answered, "check out Matthew 6:16, 25, and 31 in your Living Bible. That is My answer to you."

So I read, "And now about fasting . . . ." And I read, "Don't worry about *things*—food, drink, and clothes." And I saw I was not to worry about having enough food. Finally, the Scripture told me, "Don't be anxious about tomorrow. God will take care of your tomorrow too. Live one day at a time" (verse 34). I read this the day before my departure.

So I took *only me* to the conference. I left home at 2:00 A.M., planning to drive through the Southern California desert. Everything was fine until about 5:00 A.M. Up until then, I had sung and listened to tapes and prayed. Then I hit a heavy ground fog. I had never driven alone at night and I wondered if I would go off a cliff or if someone would rear-end me.

I slowed down to about twenty miles an hour and prayed harder (much harder) than I had before the fog. I breathed a sigh of relief when I pulled into the drive at our oldest daughter's college, just a few miles from where our conference would be, glad to squeeze in a few hours visiting with her.

Wendy, sick of dorm food, begged, "Will you take me out to breakfast, Mom?" So I took her to her favorite restaurant, several miles away. When she ordered her breakfast of steak and eggs, a thought flew through my mind: *I could have a high-protein breakfast, skip lunch, and go on to my meeting.*

God nudged me with a lively punch in the ribs. "Say, now, what have we decided about breakfast?" I remembered and ordered Sanka.

Wendy finished her meal as I drooled, and I took her back to college. After attending chapel with her, I kissed her good-bye and went to gas up the car. About twenty-five feet from a service station, my "hot" light turned bright red. I crept into the station and then it happened. My lower radiator hose blew, gushing and spewing water all over. Oh, how I praised God that I had prayed first for His protection across the desert and for His angels to drive with me. And I praised Him that I had not eaten breakfast with Wendy. If I had not returned to my favorite salad spot after leaving Wendy off at the college, I would now be sailing out on the freeway toward my conference, far from any service station.

I found my noon chef's salad superdelicious, a fine way to wait while a new radiator hose was put in my car. That was test one. The second test came when I registered at the hotel. A fancy buffet luncheon of sandwiches, potato chips, fruits, and beverages was all for the taking, but I was so full from my salad, I couldn't touch a morsel. I tucked away an apple in my purse in case I might want it later.

The hotel meals, as I had anticipated, were not dieter's fare. I picked out the protein, ate my salad and vegetables, and left everything else. The first evening, I skipped dessert and enjoyed my apple.

The next noon, when dessert was served, I asked the waiter, "Do you suppose you could find one of those juicy red apples you served yesterday?" He did.

At dinner, when I again requested fruit, he brought me two apples on a large platter, resplendent with carving knife.

By the next day I was known in the kitchen. Our waiter came up to me, winked, and whispered in my ear, "Say, we're serving lemon sherbet for dessert today. Would you prefer an apple?"

God takes care of us so beautifully! Not only did He manage my eating, but in the lobby, before we had been given our room assignments, I spotted a friend of many years, Cari. Neither of us knew the other would be coming to the conference. We embraced happily and God arranged for us to room together for the weekend. What a precious time we had.

We immediately discovered we both walk every morning and swim whenever possible. Perhaps others thought it funny to see two ladies jogging in their high heels (we hadn't planned ahead) but we thought it was fun. At 6:00 A.M. not too many people were around to observe us. We swam during all our conference breaks. The water seemed about forty degrees, cold enough to take our breath away. We felt skinnier with each of the twenty laps we swam.

I came home feeling great. Sunday morning I felt newly glamorous and thin as I dressed for church. After services, as we walked down the hallway to the car, Kermit put his arm around me.

"You're looking sexier every day," he whispered in my ear.

At dinner, which we eat at noon on Sundays, Bruce, our thirteen-year-old, asked me, "How much weight did you lose during the weekend, Mom?"

"I don't know, honey," I said. "Remember, our scales are broken."

Bruce reminded me that we had scales in the backyard. "Why don't you go weigh out there?" he asked.

Scott, eight, piped up, "That's only for the pigs!"

Kermit raises piglets in our yard (sheep, too), and that is a whole different story, which I may someday tell. But I was glad Scott did not consider me any sort of pig. (I later learned I dropped about three pounds during my energetic and obedient weekend.)

Life is not nearly so pleasant when we are disobedient. A friend, Don, weakened and bought a box of candy from a youth group on the excuse it would be a treat for his family. But he knew very well he would end up eating it all (which he did), and he deliberately ignored the prompting of the Holy Spirit to simply give a donation to the group and forget the sweets. He was furious with himself after he realized how he had given in to his own fleshly lusts—especially since he had just prayed for God to help him with his appetite.

But that trap is easy to fall into, and we must constantly be on guard. I know from a sad personal experience. Several weeks after the writers' conference, I began to feel proud of myself for being off sugars and starches for so long. Pride is dangerous.

A friend called and asked, "Have you seen the new book about a high-roughage diet? You must get a copy right away. It is terrific!"

So I jumped on my bike and hightailed it to the nearest grocery store, bought the book, and spent the day reading furiously. *Oh!* I thought, *I have somehow missed God. I am not getting nearly enough roughage in my diet*. I raced right back to the store and came home with a huge sack of unprocessed bran and some nuts.

For the next several days I faithfully took two teaspoons of bran three times a day and threw a few nuts and seeds on my salads. Pretty soon my eyes itched, my nose ran like a faucet, and my throat wanted to be scratched with a wire brush.

"God, what is this?" I asked. He must have been pleased that I finally decided to get His opinion about this new routine I had put myself on.

"Did I tell you about this program?" He gently asked. I sheepishly admitted, no. Then He reminded me of a longstanding wheat allergy. I cut the bran, and my eyes, nose, and throat returned to normal. But I was hooked on the nuts.

I reasoned that freshly roasted warm cashew nuts, though 800 calories per cup, are full of protein and good nourishment. Once again, God dealt with me. I struggled for a week to move back into obedience to the simplicity of the original plan God designed for my body: protein, fruits, and vegetables—period. Only when I moved back into total obedience did I again feel grand and begin losing more unwanted pounds.

I trust I have had enough reinforcement in one of God's principles to last me awhile: He blesses obedience. God created us with the ability to choose, and He will not interfere with our decisions. We have to decide whether we wish to obey God's instructions and reap the benefits, which are numerous, or disobey, satisfy a momentary pleasure, and hate ourselves for hours afterward.

DINNER TRIMMER

Old Mother Hubbard
Went to her cupboard
To get her fat figure a treat,

But when she got there
Her cupboard was bare
Of anything tasty to eat.

She said, "Oh, doggone!
My diet is on.
I find nothing to munch for my dinner."

Old Mother Hubbard
Shut tight her cupboard
And soon became quite a bit thinner.

9

Sugar Baby Blues

Medical science is becoming increasingly aware that, for some people, eating refined sugar is like eating poison. It upsets the body's insulin balance, triggering a craving for more and more sugar. This is true in my case. God began to show me that it would require total abstinence not only from sugar but also from refined starches, such as cereals, breads, and all processed foods. This was His method of disciplining me into appetite control and the second phase of my healing.

I am no longer one of the "average" Americans who, according to C. S. Lovett in *Jesus Wants You Well*, are consuming more than 100 pounds of white sugar every year. Since I gave up sugar entirely, I notice my nerves are 100 percent calmer, which is a blessing for a mother of four.

After I had been off refined products for a few weeks, a friend commented on my weight loss and healthy glow. She wanted to know how all this had come to pass.

I explained I had been visiting my folks in the San Francisco area and had a lot of trouble craving sweets, as usual. Mom never keeps goodies in the house and I just had to have something sweet, so I took a walk one afternoon and bought a huge double coconut cone. I was embarrassed to have anyone see me, so I scooted into a bookstore and hid. I took a lick of my cone and looked up. A book on staying slim leaped off the shelf. I finished my ice cream, bought the book, and headed home.

I told my friend, "The book explained in medical terms what refined sugars and starches were doing to my body. I began to understand that I simply cannot tolerate them. As this whole new understanding opened up, everything clicked into place for the first time. I knew I had finally been handed the key to total victory. Now I could simply relax in Jesus and watch the weight drop off. When I am absolutely obedient to Him, that is precisely what happens.

"When I received God's revelation to me, I immediately made a silent pact with Him that I would abstain from those poison foods the rest of my life if need be. My intense cravings have disappeared."

If you suspect an addictive food allergy to a particular item, it is imperative that you allow God to reveal to you the foods causing the difficulty. Then you must be willing to give those foods up. I realize that most people cannot do that in their own strength, and that is where this book, I trust, goes beyond the usual recommendations.

Chances are very good, if you are a compulsive eater, that you cannot handle refined sugars and starches. The way to find out is to eliminate them, then ledger the results. Keep track of what you eat for a while. If you binge, you must write down what triggered the binges and what you ate during that time.

Even if you have no biochemical sensitivity, the ledgering technique is helpful. If you write down what you eat, when you eat, and how you felt at the time, you can learn a lot about your eating patterns. I believe God would use this method to teach us about ourselves. If I had been more meticulous in such ledgering long ago, and more faithful in Scripture study, it's possible I would have received my healing much sooner.

I can't imagine any doctor disapproving of your eliminating poison foods from your diet. But if you have diabetes, heart trouble, or any such medical problems, you should *always* check with your physician before going on a program of any sort.

Along with writing down what you eat, when, and so on, keep track of this: What is this food doing to my body? How do I feel without it? Do I have more pep? How about sleep? Is my appetite decreasing?

Pat learned about her sugar sensitivity when she realized she was a Twinkie freak. Every day when her little girl came home from school, Pat gave her money and told her, "Run to the store and get me my box of Twinkies."

Becky got one to eat; Pat enjoyed the other eleven. She felt much too embarrassed to buy them herself. One day, a b-o-i-n-g went off inside. "God, what am I doing to You?" she asked. "How can You stand to live inside me when I cram Twinkies down in there?"

Not everyone, of course, has this problem. Susan, my pastor's wife, stayed quite heavy after her babies were born—three in a row. She leads a life which requires her to eat out constantly, mostly at the mercy of other folks' cooking. She has found that the only way she can lose weight and keep her loss under control is simply to eat no food until dinner. Then she enjoys a good portion of everything which is served. Most of us don't have Susan's ironclad willpower. But she explains, "I rely on the Lord, not myself."

God's will for us is to put into our bodies only the foods which will keep us healthy, give us vitality and energy to serve Him effectively.

SUGAR BLUES

Sugar, sugar, everywhere
I won't touch it
I don't dare!

If I take one little bite
I eat
Everything in sight.

10

One, Two!

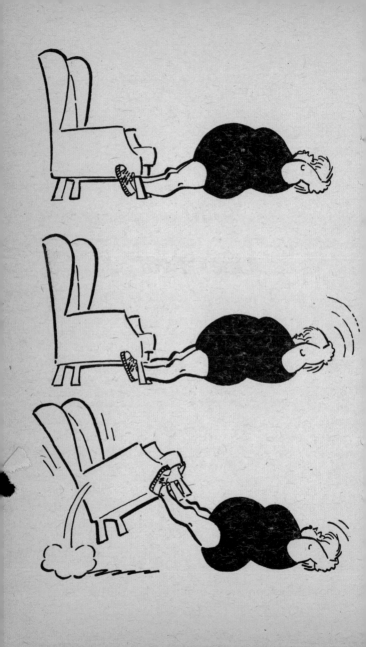

Christians sit a lot: in church, prayer meetings, Bible studies, and at ice-cream socials. As a Christian I found myself getting fatter than ever from lack of exercise and such good fellowship in food.

After my healing from compulsive eating, I prayed, "O Lord, I'm still flabby and sluggish. Do something! I don't know what would be best for me."

About a week later, He sent me a new friend. Jean teaches physical fitness at our local junior college. Soon she was on my family-room floor, every rubberized inch of her, demonstrating what she felt would be best for me. She had me lie flat on my back, arms to the sides. Then I was to draw my knees to my chest, hold them tightly there and do fifty rolls on my hips, each side counting half a roll.

Next, Jean had me put my feet under the couch and do ten sit-ups for my flabby belly. It took about fifteen minutes to finish the routine. Then she told me, "I want you to walk briskly each day, covering at least a mile and a half in half an hour."

I got busy. God began waking me up about 3:30 A.M., and I bumped and rolled the first thing. Then, as soon as daylight broke, I walked, followed by barking neighborhood dogs. I learned what routes to take to avoid being bitten. I don't know why God woke me so early at first, unless He knew that was how to get me into a good routine. Now I run in spurts, sometimes sleeping until 5:30 or even later. On my walks, I pray first, about fifteen minutes, then try to be quiet and listen to God the other half of the time.

After I got off all sugar/flour, I indulged in exercise like a maniac. Remarkably—fat, lazy, sluggish me began to *crave* exercise. I try, but I don't always succeed, to force myself to ride my ancient seven-dollar bike the half mile to the grocery store instead of hopping into my car.

I feel like Paul must have felt—yes, that's it— running a good, hard race: "Like an athlete I punish my body, treating it roughly, training it to do what it should, not what it wants to. Otherwise I fear that after enlisting others for the race, I myself might be declared unfit and ordered to stand aside"(1 Corinthians 9:27).

As Harriet LaBarre explains in the *Family Circle* article "Dr. Kremer's No Hunger Diet," exercise decreases your appetite by stimulating your fat cells to release their stored fat, giving you added energy and boosting your feeling of well-being.

Just think! All those millions of body cells formerly neglected from sitting around can finally come to life through the oxygen you will now send to them through your exercise program. Your circulation will improve. Buoyant health can be yours as you discipline yourself into a program of physical fitness. There are any number of ways to do it. Walking is cheap, convenient, and anyone can participate. One of my friends, Jo, puts her baby in the carriage and walks to the store or to church. Doris walks to work.

Many cities have recreation exercise programs, but our local one was too time-consuming for me and didn't capture my interest. I tried tennis and was a real dud at it. Then I discovered that I excel at swimming, so I do lots of that in season. I wish I were a jogger, because jogging burns up a lot of calories quickly (ten calories per minute)— then the day's exercise is finished. But I can go only about a half block before I'm panting for dear life, so I do that and then walk the rest of the way. If you can jog your mile, you may call yourself blessed.

I think the only way to keep at a regular exercise program is to find out what you enjoy and can do halfway decently, then find what fits into your schedule and way of life, and do it consistently. There's no point in choosing an activity you detest. Be ingenious. Use your imagination to create exercise opportunities and you will find ways to burn extra calories.

FITNESS FINISH

Today, perhaps I'll do my bit
About becoming physically fit.
It's plain to see I'm far too ample
Which does not set a good example.

I've thought before of trimming
With some concentrated swimming.
I've considered miles of jogging
For cholesterol unclogging.
I restored my ancient bike
And arranged to take a hike.
I even bought a tennis racquet and
Signed up for lessons, but couldn't hack it.

But the exercise that works the best
Is far more simple than all the rest.
I push myself away from the table
As fast and as far as I am able.

11

Fasting

Fasting enthusiasts tell us we feel better physically, mentally, and spiritually when we fast because it cleans out our systems. The Bible mentions fasting seventy-four times, in many forms and for many reasons.

I feel it is dangerous for people to go on an extended fast blithely, without medical approval. This is especially true if there is any history of hypoglycemia, diabetes, or other physical problem. Don't attempt such a fast unless God speaks to your heart (with inner conviction and peace) and tells you to do so.

I jumped into such a program without praying about it first. I had read Frances Hunter's book *God's Answer to Fat . . . Loøse It!*, which I feel has much to offer. Many have felt led to try a "Daniel" fast (*see* Daniel 1:12), which allows only vegetables and water for ten days. Because I wanted to achieve immediate success, I ignored past low-blood-sugar problems and tried this program. Many others have had tremendous suc-

cess with it, but I felt icy cold, listless and miserable.

Stubbornly, I stuck out the diet, only to regain
immediately the few pounds I had lost. I did not
feel human again until I added protein back to
my diet. Now I know enough to stop a fast if I feel
freezing cold and exhausted. I don't try to make a
fetish out of letting God know how good I am at
fasting.

God put Jamie Buckingham, Christian writer,
on a twenty-eight-day fast which started him on
crucifying his flabby flesh. Another friend,
Marge, felt led to go to a particular medical
specialist before fasting. Her Spirit-filled Christian doctor, being cautious, required all sorts of
tests, including a glucose tolerance, before he
would allow her to fast. Now she has only water
on Mondays and Thursdays, fasting for purposes
of losing weight.

Other folk, like my diabetic friend Kay, can get
into trouble with fasting one meal. Her doctor
has her diet and medication balanced for the
sugar level that she needs to maintain. Fasting
upsets this delicate insulin balance.

So we are back to the *individual you*. Although
fasting is not easy for me, there are times I feel
led to fast a meal in addition to my breakfast.
When I do, I offer this as a sacrifice to the Lord,
thanking Him for helping me to bring my appetite totally under subjection to His Spirit.

I'm not one to fast for the sake of fasting. I
believe we should know why we are doing it.
Fasting should be done in obedience to God, to
cleanse your system, for intercessory prayer, in
agreement with friends, or however God directs.
The time one normally would eat should be
given to God in prayer.

I recommend that you read *God's Chosen Fast*
by Arthur Wallis (listed in bibliographical section) for an extensive biblical study of the subject. He discusses not only various types of fasts
but also the reasons God gives for fasting and
how to go about it.

Fasting, for me, seems to be a form of releasing
my flesh to the Spirit's control, a process of dying
to self. Isaiah 58:6 reads: "Is not this the fast that
I have chosen? to loose the bands of wickedness,
to undo the heavy burdens, and to let the op-
pressed go free, and that ye break every yoke?"
(KJV).

Controlling the terrible compulsive cravings I
had for sugars and starches is not difficult now.
Perhaps being so aware of the damage one bite
does to me is motivation enough for abstinence.
But I have not been so absolutely perfect in listening to God's voice on some of the other foods,
such as cheddar cheese. I found myself eating
four or five ounces a day, which can run over five
hundred calories. Eliminating those calories
would mean losing up to two pounds a week.
When I reached a standstill on weight loss and

asked God for help again, I received a check from the Holy Spirit on the cheese. I tried prayer and poring over Scripture, but it was not until I agreed to forgo cheese for a week that I was released from the bondage I found myself coming into.

There is no doubt that a twenty-four-hour fast will quickly tell you what priority your appetite takes. After being off all sugar and starch for a month, I figured (I used to hate that word, but it grows sweeter each day) I could whip through such a fast like a breeze.

I began with a good, solid breakfast of broiled meat, cottage cheese, and two fruits. This I did despite the fact that I usually go light on breakfast. I just wasn't ready to accept that my breakfast meal belonged totally to God.

By noon I was famished, my stomach sounding like a barrel organ. I fixed a teaspoon of bouillon and, with the help of a two-hour nap to make it through, managed until suppertime. Then I had to fortify myself with tea.

I had wanted to prove to God that food no longer controlled me; I discovered—and He probably smiled over it—that I have a long way yet to go. But I felt the discipline was good for me, a sacrifice to God of something important in my life.

I prayed, "Lord, I'm sick and tired of food having *any* control over me, and I give You my appetite totally." So He was in the whole thing, but I still found myself becoming prouder as the day wore on. Our all-knowing God apparently knew my self-esteem needed a boost, and He was gracious to see me through the day.

The next morning, I woke up feeling downright skinny, instead of like the great white whale. I was in my son's room making the bed when I heard a faith call, "Evelyn, Evelyn . . . ."

I was sure it wasn't God, but I couldn't imagine who it could be. Then I peeked out Scott's window and spotted Olive, my next-door neighbor, crouched behind her car in the driveway.

"Why, Olive!" I called. "Whatever is the matter?"

"Any of your kids home?" she asked. "I locked myself out of the house and this bedroom window is the only one unlocked." She pointed about six feet above the car and added, "I'm too big to crawl through it."

"The children are gone," I offered, "but I'm quite sure I can be of help. I'll be right over."

I had wondered why Olive was hiding behind the car. Now I noticed she had on a sheer nightie. "Guess you're glad you won't have to call a locksmith, eh?" I commented. Then I studied the window.

Not only was it six feet high, it was one and one half feet square. Sucking in my belly, I climbed onto Olive's car, scooted through the window and onto a high dresser, leaped down onto her bed, and sprinted to the door to open it for her. Although this incident boosted my morale, there are far more profound benefits from fasting than being able to squeeze through a small window.

Fasting, as I mentioned, can help break a compulsive eating pattern. It is also a good way to break a plateau. If you haven't dropped any weight for a couple of weeks, a twenty-four- to forty-eight-hour water fast will do wonders to get the fat burning again.

We have spoken mostly of self-centered reasons for fasting, to benefit ourselves. Fasting is also ordained by God as a means of intercessory prayer. We seem to come into a deeper awareness of God's presence and purposes and can often pray more effectively for others when we are fasting.

Edie, a minister's wife, was stricken with encephalitis and fell into a deep coma. Doctors feared she would either die or be a vegetable all her life. God instructed two couples to spend three days on a water fast, praying for Edie's healing. At the end of their fast, Edie was instantly healed and is today the picture of health.

If you wish to gain spiritual strength to fight life's battles for yourself and for others, if you desire to draw closer to God—try fasting.

LASTING AT FASTING?

Fasting leaves the tummy with
A mighty empty feeling.
Just how long you stick it out
Is certainly revealing.

Do you moan and groan and growl
And feel that you are dying?
Or do you say, "Well! Praise the Lord!"
And make a stab at trying?

12

Think, Eat, and Be Merry

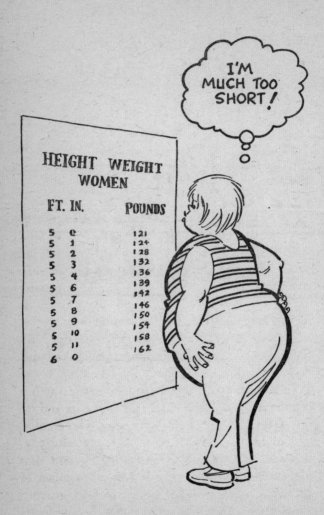

Now that we've talked about your being God's project, accepting yourself, learning how God will bring deliverance to your body, crucifying your flesh, hearing God, biochemical sensitivities, and fasting, let's talk about our intellect. God wants us to use it. "He who guards his mouth keeps his life, but he who opens wide his lips will come to ruin" (Proverbs 13:3 AMPLIFIED). It takes thinking to guard our mouths.

There is quite a difference between using our intellect to obey what God has shown us and relying solely upon human reasoning. God created us so that we are forced to make choices. Whenever we have a food choice—and that means every meal, every business breakfast or luncheon, every social occasion and grocery shopping—we are obligated to choose the foods that will give our bodies the best in nutrition so that we can function at maximum efficiency.

Not only have I been guilty of eating badly for years, but worse yet, that's how I fed my family. I have allowed such horrors as greasy potato chips, sugary cookies, white bread, and quick-food items in my pantry. Now we have switched to grainy brown bread, fresh fruit, cheese, nuts, raisins, dates, and seeds. I won't lie and say I have had complete cooperation, but I am trying to be firm and consistent. We are making progress. How can we expect much from God if we go to the store and come home with empty-caloried junk foods?

It is wise to study the caloric content of various foods, without becoming fanatical. Avoid foods loaded with fats and carbohydrates. There is a list of the calories in the proteins, fruits, and vegetables that I use in the cooking section (Chapter 14) of this book.

God does not want us blithely eating away, unaware of what our bodies are consuming, nor does He want us so bound by a particular system that we are terribly rigid about the whole thing.

I do not like to get into methodology for one reason: I want you to seek God for yourself and not look to the eating methods of anyone else. What is best for one person is not necessarily best for you. Yet I realize many do not know where to begin, and need some guidelines. I am always curious to know what works for others, and if you weren't seeking help, you would not be reading this book. So I will share with you now how God is working with me.

I limit my foods, basically, to three groups:

Proteins:	meat, fish, fowl, eggs, milk, cheese, cottage cheese
Fruits:	fresh, whenever possible, or water pack
Vegetables:	fresh and raw, if possible

I eat no corn and rarely a baked potato, because they seem too starchy for my system and trigger desire for more. However, since they are whole-some foods, I would not suggest that you elimi-nate them entirely without first experimenting and seeing what they do to your body. God is also speaking to many of His people about including natural grains in their eating, so check this out with Him. I have not felt led to add them to my program, but this does not mean they are not for you.

The mainstay of my eating program is *salad*, loaded with raw vegetables and dressed lightly. I am sick of oil and vinegar, but I enjoy ranch-style dressing mix, made with buttermilk and imita-tion mayonnaise, so that is what I have most often. I was treating myself to blue cheese on my restaurant salads, but it became nauseating after a while (too thick and goopy). If I know ahead I will be eating out, I take along a little two-ounce vial of my own dressing.

My doctor fully approves of my eating plan, and he told me, "I think anyone who is overweight makes a mistake eating breakfast." I know other doctors who would strongly disagree with such a statement, but that was God's word to me, using my doctor as His mouthpiece. I have sadly learned that if I wake up with growls and gurgles and indulge in breakfast, I'm a lot hungrier by noon than if I had fasted the morning meal. Notice I said *fasted*, not skipped. Skipping meals is something you do in your own strength. Fasting you offer to the Lord as a means of disciplining your appetite.

I was eating too much at bedtime, sometimes cheese and nuts and raisins. This habit began when I tried the high-roughage program for a week. That little inner voice of the Lord said, "Cut it!" and it took fasting to break the routine.

Sometimes I have to *think* not to eat, as old habits take time to break and new ones even longer to establish. Basically, God has me on two meals a day. Usually when I eat more, the Holy Spirit lets me know I am yielding to fleshly cravings. I like Frances Hunter's suggestion in her book *God's Answer to Fat . . . Loose It!* that we ask, "*Jesus, how little can I get by with?*" Make it a challenge to see how few calories can fill you. Work at putting your appetite to death.

When I plan something for the family which I

feel is not for me, I seek God's guidance. I might end up with just a small protein salad while they enjoy homemade spaghetti. It doesn't bother them and it is fine with me. In fact, tonight I fixed them pork spareribs in my slow cooker (we raised our own pig last year), baked potatoes, vegetables, salad, and fruit. I baked myself a skinny chicken breast and had it with carrots, cauliflower, and green salad. (Each time I combat eating what I shouldn't, it destroys old desires and strengthens the new. It makes me feel all warm and successful inside.)

After the evening's dinner, my husband said, "Come sit," and patted his lap. Since we've been married twenty years and he has never done that before, I was puzzled. He kissed me, as Scott watched wide-eyed, and he said, "I told one of my classes a little about our intimate life today."

He had taken our sheepskin rug to demonstrate to his agriculture class how the sheep are sheared so that a certain amount of nap is left, then how the rugs are treated by an electrical process, and dyed into any color desired. I wondered what on earth the connection might be between the rug and our deep secrets, which he had apparently divulged to an entire class of teenagers.

"I showed the rug to them," he said, "and told them I brought it home to you as a 'just because' present."

Kermit continued, "Their eyes and ears perked up and I told them, 'just because I love her.' "

"Is that *all* you told them?" I asked.

"Sure," he replied. "What did you think?" Then he added, "You are looking great. I *like* your new figure." Then he planted a second kiss on my nose as Scott smiled.

So it pays to *think* before you eat. *Think* of all the rewards.

Make it a rule, especially, to think when you are out or traveling. Chef's salads with dressing on the side are always a safe bet and I adore them. If you go to someone's home, you can usually pick at meat or salad and make out, even though you may have to go home hungry.

Think hard before you ever blurt out "I'm on a diet!" That's like a red flag to a bull; and friends and foe alike will fight you tooth and nail. Just say "I'm allergic," or whatever. By the time it registers, you can gather your defenses for the battle.

A while back, I wrote down everything I ate for a few days. I was curious to see how it all added up. I found out about some fleshly mistakes I needed to correct.

SIX-DAY WAR

Sunday Breakfast: FAST.

Lunch: Crockpot dinner: small hunk roast, carrots, onion.

Green beans seasoned with onion salt and a squirt of liquid oleomargarine.

Lettuce, tomato, pepper salad with oil/vinegar.

Cooked cabbage with squirt of oleo.

Dinner: Small carton of chive cottage cheese.

Apple.

Monday Breakfast: 4 ounces orange juice.

Lunch: Small lean hamburger patty with slice of tomato, onion, and melted cheese on top.

Green beans with squirt of oleo.

Dinner: ½ cup cottage cheese.

Small lettuce, tomato, pepper salad.

Peas with oleo.

Small wedge watermelon.

Tuesday Breakfast: FAST.

Lunch: Lettuce, tomato, crabmeat (4 ounces), apple salad with diet mayonnaise.

Tuesday	Midafternoon:	Pear.
	Dinner:	Broiled burger patty with onion, tomato, and cheese.
		Peas and oleo.
		Apple.
Wednesday	Breakfast:	4 ounces orange juice.
		Apple.
		2 ounces cheese.
	Lunch:	Lettuce salad.
	(out)	Diet jello with tuna.
		Cottage cheese with water-pack pineapple.
	Dinner:	Burger patty with onion, tomato, and cheese.
Thursday	Breakfast:	Orange.
	Lunch:	Lettuce salad with dressing.
	(out)	Cottage cheese.
		Carrot salad, cabbage salad, beets and celery.
Friday	Breakfast:	FAST.
	Lunch:	½ cup each: cottage cheese, water-pack pineapple.
	Dinner:	Skinny skinned chicken breast, baked with onion.
		Carrots, cauliflower.
		Lettuce salad with oil/vinegar.

Note:
Daily caloric average: 850.

I learned during those six days that I can go to a baby shower and not indulge in decorated cake, ice cream, punch, or mints. Iced tea *can* satisfy!

I also found out I could enjoy two luncheons and not overdo. Since those few days, God has put me on the breakfast fast. I was quite fleshly Wednesday morning of that week, knowing I would have lunch out, and I fortified myself with a good breakfast. Obviously I was thinking far too much about what maybe I might have to do without at noon. I have pretty well progressed beyond that stage. I now go to luncheons—lots of them—with the attitude that God will show me what I may have; and if it is zero, so be it. He has proved faithful every time to meet my needs.

I feel totally relaxed now about eating out. I don't count every little calorie and I don't spend all day stewing about what I will eat. I am no longer, praise God forever, *obsessed* with food. I have absolute trust, finally, that God will provide for my needs and I just relax in Him. He has waited a long time for me to progress this far, believe me.

If you will concentrate on proteins (3- or 4-ounce portions), vegetables, and some fruit, you will probably find your appetite regulating itself and your food needs decreasing. If you aren't losing one or two pounds (or more) a week, it might be wise to ledger your food for a few days and get a realistic idea of how many calories

you are putting into your mouth. My doctor feels
1000 or so for a woman, more for a man, should
be plenty to cover one's nutritional needs. (One
week I ate 600 calories a day or so of cheese and
nuts on top of my regular meals. No wonder I
didn't lose any weight.)

There is no getting around the fact that the
fewer calories we eat and the more we burn
through vigorous exercise, the faster we will trim
down. How quickly calories are used varies with
individuals as well as with activities. No two
people will lose at the same rate on the same
program, and daily use also varies. For instance,
today I typed all day, a sedentary activity. Tomorrow I will strip beds, wash, clean, do
yardwork, and, I hope, burn up a couple of
pounds' worth.

You might also want to know what your ideal
weight should be, though I imagine most of our
doctors have told us several times what they wish
we weighed. I am giving you a height-weight
chart here. Please remember that these are
generous averages and you may need to be ten
pounds lighter or heavier, depending on your
bones and the weight at which you feel most
energetic and alive. Let's be realistic, though,
and not call ourselves large boned when we
aren't at all. Nor should our goal be to resemble a
toothpick.

This chart goes by ordinary clothing (about five

pounds of it) and no shoes. If you weigh twenty
pounds above the listed figures, you are probably
overweight. Usually, all you have to do is look in
a mirror to know that, anyway.

HEIGHT-WEIGHT CHART

HEIGHT		WOMEN	MEN
Ft.	In.	Pounds	Pounds
4	8	112	
4	9	114	
4	10	116	
4	11	118	
5	0	121	126
5	1	124	129
5	2	128	132
5	3	132	135
5	4	136	139
5	5	139	142
5	6	142	146
5	7	146	150
5	8	150	154
5	9	154	158
5	10	158	162
5	11	162	166
6	0	166	172
6	1		178
6	2		184
6	3		190

We are not to be all hung up on how fast the outer shell is falling off, but we do need to be concerned with how obedient we are being to God. We can measure our progress by our ability to lose interest in the importance we give to food in our lives.

You will need to experiment and really pray and seek God until you find your own niche. *Think* first, then eat. You will be far happier.

You remember the well-known prayer: "God, grant me the serenity to accept the things I cannot change; the courage to change the things I can; and the wisdom to know the difference." I have written what I feel is applicable to my life and will share it with you. Why don't you try writing your own thoughts under each category?

- *God, grant me the serenity to accept the things I cannot change:*
  God has told me my discipline lies in total abstinence from sugar and starches. I praise God that I can live, and live well, on protein, fruit, and vegetables, which are far more healthful. I *cannot* change the fact that sugar/starches trigger compulsive eating for me, so I accept that and praise God for revealing it to me after such a long search for answers. I *cannot* change the fact that if I am disobedient to what God has revealed to me about my body, I will reap what I sow and suffer the consequences: sluggishness, fat,

guilt, self-consciousness, and a poor Christian witness.

- *The courage to change the things I can:*
  I *can* learn to eat what God tells me is okay for my body, what my body needs for the best of health. I *can* change my disobedience into obedience to God through Jesus Christ, who gives me the strength to do so. I *can* change the eating habits of my family as well as my own eating habits, giving better health for all. I *can* strip the house of junk foods. I *can* insist my family eat properly, for it is my responsibility as a wife and mother.

  I *can* force myself into exercise each day, even if I don't want to. I *can* do it as unto the Lord. I *can* change my poor self-image, and I *can* allow God to develop latent talents for His glory. I *can* learn to receive myself. There are lots of things I *can* do.

- *And the wisdom to know the difference:*
  It is my privilege as a child of God to ask for His divine wisdom, for the Mind of Christ. I simply pray, "Lord Jesus, help me to rest in You. Show me what I must accept as facts of life, direct me to change what You want changed. I yield to You. Show me the unique and personal plan You have for my life, so that my living may bring glory to Your name."

You, too, can be set free from your fat by the power of God. He will give you a new song to sing, of praises to Him. And a new figure to enjoy.

THINK, EAT, AND BE MERRY

Eat, drink, and be merry
For tomorrow you may die.
The one who penned this sage advice
Did not tell a lie.

But THINK, eat, and be merry,
You'll soon feel fit and trim.
I guarantee, you'll come alive,
Your grim will change to vim.

13

Afterglow

Before, when I was obsessed either with being heavy or with a rigid diet program, I was so totally absorbed in it that I was a nervous wreck over the whole affair. The moment I lost an ounce (I weighed four or five times a day if I was being "good") I madly tried on all my clothes to see how *everything* fit. This whole system of Jesus being in control is entirely different. I feel all quiet inside, a real miracle for hyperactive me. A friend told me I have a new "softness." Now, as clothes become baggy, I simply give them away or put them into my cedar chest for later remodeling. When Jesus finishes with my exterior, I'll look them over again.

I have followed His instructions to get rid of my sombers (I look dead in black, gray, and dark green) and to emerge, instead, like a bright butterfly. I found time to whip up a shocking pink suit which cost me less than five dollars to create. I no longer feel I must hide in my cocoon, but rather enjoy the metamorphosis which has taken

place in my body and in my feelings about myself.

One of the transformations I find is a new release to be able to listen—really listen—to my
family, friends, and strangers. Before, I was so
obsessed with my own problem, it blocked my
sensitivity to others. I was embarrassed about
myself and my body, which inhibited my ability
to reach out to others in a free flow of love.

When we come into self-acceptance through
Jesus and find success in Him, we begin a new
other-centeredness. Our attitude becomes, How
can I get to know Peg (or Stan or whoever) and
the things which are important to her (or him)?
How can we share these interests? New empathy
and compassion for others develop. This is Jesus'
kind of unconditional love flowing through us.

Tell me, can you find that in any man-made
system of weight control?

HOW ABOUT YOU?

I'd like to hear your ditty,
My brain has run quite dry.
Share with me *your* wisdom,
Please give it a try.

Send it care of the publisher.
He will forward it here.
Someday, you just never know,
It may, in print, appear.

14

Combat Cooking

Combat cooking is for all of us enlisted in the Battle of the Bulge. We want to concentrate our forces on proteins, vegetables, and fruits. We must fortify ourselves against the onslaught of our enemy by keeping reserve forces on hand. How about preparing your own two-week Battle Plan based on the suggested recipes? Or, plan some combinations of your own.

All recipes are geared to serve four persons. I personally like to double such foods as meat loaves and put one portion in the freezer. This saves a lot of time and energy for the next round.

I am giving you a list of the caloric value of various foods in each cooking section. For a more complete listing, you might wish to purchase a calorie counter at your nearby drugstore.

I am also giving you a basic menu plan.

Happy slimming!

BASIC MENU PLAN

Breakfast: FAST.
(Note: If you are led to eat breakfast, I suggest a small portion of protein and a citrus fruit.)

Lunch: About 4 cups of lettuce and other raw vegetables with about 4 ounces of canned fish, cottage cheese, or other protein as desired.
Fruit, if desired.

Dinner: 4 to 6 ounces of protein from one of the recipes given.
2 or more cups of raw vegetable salad.
½ to 1 cup other vegetable.
Fresh fruit.

Bedtime: Tomato juice, if desired.

I often eat the dinner at noon and have just a salad in the evening, depending upon how hungry I am and what I plan for dinner for the rest of the family. If you eat dinner at noon, it works well to fast the evening meal if led to do so.

I do not drink coffee, as caffeine accentuates low-blood-sugar problems and also makes me very jumpy. But I do indulge in weak tea and diet sodas.

PROTEIN PLUS

Protein keeps our energy levels up and hunger pangs down. It is easy to get in a rut and serve the same thing over and over, which is great if it doesn't bore either you or your family. But most of us enjoy variety, so here are several ideas. The calorie count is at the end of the section.

Remember, your barbecue is a good friend and you can cook about anything outside: frankfurters, chicken, steak, chops. If you have a rotisserie, you have even more choices, such as turkey and roasts.

Weather bad? Try all of the above in your broiler. When you roast, use a rack so fat drips away. Try to avoid frying. It adds lots of needless calories and is not healthful.

CHICKEN LITTLE

Cut up and skin a fryer chicken or parts. Dip in evaporated skim milk and roll in wheat germ. Lay pieces on foil. Bake on cookie sheet, 45 minutes, 350°.

For variety, try sprinkling your skinned chicken with onion flakes and chicken bouillon. Wrap tightly in foil before baking. 400° for 45 minutes.

Chicken is also delicious when you roast it in your slow cooker. You can make chicken soup the second day from the broth.

FISH TALES

Cook as Chicken Little, but only for 20 minutes, at 400°.

Take a can of salmon, tuna, or crab. Mix with capers, onion, and a little imitation mayonnaise. Put in baking dish. Add sliced tomato and cheese. Bake 20 minutes, 350°.

LIVER BY SELMA

(The very thought of liver used to make me quiver.
Then I tried this recipe. Not bad, occasionally.)

Scald liver. (Personally, lamb liver is what I like, as the flavor is mild.) Take a Teflon frying pan and add 2 ounces bouillon, 1/3 cup water, and stir. Sauté your meat in this liquid and then take it out and set aside while you prepare the sauce.

SAUCE: Put into frying pan, 1 cup tomato juice, 1 tablespoon dried onion flakes, 4 shakes each garlic powder and seasoned salt. Cook on medium heat until it comes to a boil, then turn down to simmer. It will thicken by itself without adding any thickening agent. After about 15 minutes, add a can of mushrooms (juice and all) or fresh mushrooms. Cook some more. Then add liver and cook about 5 minutes. Serve with lemon juice.

MEATY LOAF

Mix 2 pounds lean ground beef, 1 egg, ¼ cup bran (optional) and seasonings: celery, thyme, onion, seasoned salt. Shape into loaf and place on broiler pan. Bake 1 hour, 350°. You can add dry powdered skim milk to your meat for added protein, if desired.

OBOY OMELET

Beat 4 eggs. Grate some cheese (about ½ cup) and chop ¼ cup onion and green pepper. Lightly butter omelet pan or frying pan. Add eggs. After they set, add other ingredients. Fold over. Enjoy.

REGAL ROAST

Our favorite Sunday dinner is the one I throw into my slow cooker Saturday evening.

Peel potatoes and cut into slices. Put in bottom of slow cooker. Add onion, carrots, and about ¼ cup water. Season roast and stick in pot. Turn it all on low about 10:00 P.M. Saturday evening. Eat anytime Sunday. Supplement with green vegetable, salad, and fruit.

SWELL SOUP

We love homemade soup. When I roast a turkey or chicken, I make soup from the broth. And

Monday night I use any broth and leftovers from our Sunday roast to create soup.

First, I cook any bones, adding water and seasonings of bay leaf, salt, pepper, onion. After a couple of hours, I strain and chill the broth. When it is cold, I skim off any fat. Then I add fresh carrots, celery, tomato or tomato juice, and a couple of bouillon cubes. It is simple to do all this in a slow cooker, but you can use a standard pot.

TACO SALAD

Brown 1½ pounds lean ground beef and set aside. Prepare family-size salad of lettuce, tomato, onion, and 1 small can drained kidney beans. Toss with oil and vinegar dressing.

Divide into four bowls or plates. Add meat and top with grated cheese. For nondieters, add crushed taco chips on top. (You can make this ahead in a casserole-type vessel and take to potlucks.)

TOP HAT BURGERS

Shape one beef patty for each person and broil or pan fry on one side. Broil 3 minutes on second side. Top each patty with a slice of onion, tomato, and cheese. Broil until cheese melts. If you pan fry, cook on second side a few minutes, put lid on pan and steam about 4 minutes more. Serve with vegetable salad and fruit.

TURKEY TREAT

You can use ground turkey as you would beef, but it has far fewer calories. Sometimes it is hard to buy. I get mine in 10-pound lots at a locker plant and have them cut it into 2-pound packages.

Mix 2 pounds raw turkey, 1 teaspoon chicken bouillon, and 1 egg. Shape into small balls and broil to brown. Put 1 quart tomato juice into your slow cooker or pot on stove. Add garlic salt, onion, minced celery, green pepper, fresh mushrooms, and bay leaf. Put browned turkey balls into the sauce and turn it all on low. I make this a day ahead.

PROTEIN CALORIES

From *Nutritive Value of Foods*, United States Department of Agriculture Home and Garden Bulletin No. 72.

FOOD ITEM	AMOUNT	CALORIES
BEEF		
Pot roast	3 oz.	245
Lean hamburger	3 oz.	185
Oven roast	3 oz.	375
Steak, broiled	3 oz.	220–300
CHICKEN		
Flesh only	3 oz.	115
(baked or broiled)		

FOOD ITEM	AMOUNT	CALORIES
FISH		
Most fillets	3 oz.	135
Crab	3 oz.	85
Salmon	3 oz.	120
Shrimp	3 oz.	100
Tuna	3 oz.	170
FRANKFURTERS	1	170
LAMB		
Thick broiled chop	1	400
Leg	3 oz.	235
LIVER	4 oz.	230
PORK		
Lean ham	3 oz.	245
Chop	thick	260
Roast	3 oz.	310
VEAL		
1 cutlet	3 oz.	185

VEGETABLE VARIETY

Vegetables provide good roughage and are low in calories. Eat lots of them!

Raw-vegetable salads fill you up and keep you feeling satisfied, if supplemented with moderate amounts of protein.

You might use lettuce, tomato, red cabbage, cucumber, green pepper, cauliflower, onion, carrots, celery, radish, and fresh mushrooms all in one salad.

When I cook vegetables, I use as little liquid as possible in order to retain vitamins. We enjoy a little melted cheese on top of broccoli, squash, cauliflower, or asparagus.

Try using a little minced onion flakes and imitation butter seasoning to add flavor to your cooking. I also like a squirt of liquid oleomargarine on my vegetables, but I am sparing.

Use variety to get more vitamins and minerals into your system.

HORS D'OEUVRES

1. Select large mushrooms and pull out the stems. Save for cooking later in other recipes. Stuff each mushroom cap with tuna, cottage cheese, or cheddar cheese. Pop under broiler until brown. Serve with chilled tomato juice.

2. Prepare a dip of cottage cheese or imitation sour cream. Serve with fresh vegetables: pepper and celery spears, carrot sticks, cucumber, raw cauliflower, radishes, and mushrooms.

TOMATOES AND ONIONS

Parboil fresh onions and place in baking dish. Top with fresh tomatoes or tomato soup, undiluted. Bake 30 minutes at 350°.

VEGETABLE LIST AND CALORIES

From *Nutritive Value of Foods*, United States Department of Agriculture Home and Garden Bulletin No. 72.

All calories listed are for 1-cup portions, unless otherwise indicated.

FOOD ITEM	CALORIES
Asparagus, cooked, drained	30
Beets	55
Broccoli	40
Brussels sprouts	55
Cabbage	20
Carrots	45
Cauliflower	25
Celery	15
Cucumber (1)	30
Lettuce (head)	30
Mushrooms	40
Okra	25
Peas	115*
Peppers	15
Radishes (1)	1
Sour pickles (1)	10
String beans	30
Summer squash	30
Tomatoes	30
Tomato juice	45
Winter squash	130*
Zucchini	30

* If you can survive without peas and winter squash, so much the better. They are very high in carbohydrates.

FRUIT FUN

I often serve fresh fruit salad for my family. I use the basics of apple, orange, banana, and either fresh pineapple in season or water-pack pineapple. I add other fruits as available and use no dressing.

If you enjoy being fancy, try cutting a pineapple or watermelon in half and use it as a salad boat. Great for company.

Get in the habit of serving fresh fruit for your family desserts—just a selection of in-season fruits in a pretty bowl.

One other company suggestion by my friend Kay: When melons and pineapple are in season, cut into spears and serve with toothpicks on a pretty tray. She uses this to complement chicken dishes especially.

FRUIT CALORIES

From *Nutritive Value of Foods,* United States Department of Agriculture Home and Garden Bulletin No. 72.

FRUIT	AMOUNT	CALORIES
Apple	1, raw	70
Apricots	3	55
Banana	1	100
Berries	1 cup	85
Cantaloupe	½	60
Cherries	1 cup	105

FRUIT	AMOUNT	CALORIES
Dates	1 cup	490
Fig	1 large	60
Grapes	1 cup	65
Grapefruit	½	45
Orange	1	65
Peach	1	35
Pear	1	100
Pineapple	1 cup	85
Plum	1	25
Prunes	4	70
Raisins	½ ounce	40
Tangerine	1	40
Watermelon	4- by 8-inch wedge	115

MISCELLANEOUS ITEM CALORIES

Bran flakes	1 cup	105
Butter, oils	1 tablespoon	100
Mayonnaise	1 tablespoon	100
Honey	1 tablespoon	65

LOW-CALORIE DIET

Monday Breakfast: WEAK TEA.
Lunch: 1 bouillon cube in ½ cup diluted water.
Dinner: 3 drops prune juice (GARGLE ONLY).

Tuesday	Breakfast:	Scraped crumbs from burnt toast.
	Lunch:	1 doughnut hole (WITHOUT SUGAR).
		1 glass dehydrated water.
	Dinner:	3 grains cornmeal, broiled.
Wednesday	Breakfast:	Boiled-out stains of tablecloth cover.
	Lunch:	½ dozen poppy seeds.
	Dinner:	Bee's knees and mosquito knuckles sautéd with vinegar.
Thursday	Breakfast:	Shredded eggshell skins.
	Lunch:	Boiled peach fuzz from one small peach.
	Dinner:	Filet of soft-shell crab claw.
Friday	Breakfast:	2 lobster antennae.
	Lunch:	1 guppy fin.
	Dinner:	3 eyes from Irish potato (diced).
Saturday	Breakfast:	4 chopped banana seeds.
	Lunch:	Broiled butterfly livers.
	Dinner:	Jellyfish vertebrae à la Bookbinder.
Sunday	Breakfast:	Pickled hummingbird tongue.
	Lunch:	Prime ribs of tadpole.
	Dinner:	Aroma of empty custard-pie plate.
		Tossed paprika and cloverleaf (1) salad.

Note:

All meals to be eaten under microscope to avoid extra portions.

15

The Living Word

I have tried to pull out Scripture for you which I find particularly helpful in the Battle of the Bulge. This is only a tiny fragment of the riches available in God's Word. I suggest you begin your own notebook, and every time you read a passage which God brings to life for you in relation to your problem, write it down, memorize it. Then call upon those promises of God in times of stress for edification.

You might even consider buying a paperback Bible and marking in yellow every passage which helps you fight your battle. Use this specifically for your weight-control program.

I have used the following abbreviations: LB for The Living Bible, KJV for King James Version, AMPLIFIED for Amplified version. Perhaps you may want to check these Scriptures in several versions to see how they speak to your heart.

Psalm 40 should apply to all of us, now that we are coming to the end of this book. Let me share it with you, verses 1 to 3, from The Living Bible:

I waited patiently for God to help me; then he listened and heard my cry. He lifted me out of the pit of despair, out from the bog and the mire, and set my feet on a hard, firm path and steadied me as I walked along. He has given me a new song to sing, of praises to our God. Now many will hear of the glorious things he did for me, and stand in awe before the Lord, and put their trust in him.

THE LIVING WORD

Old Testament

Leviticus 26:13 LB	For I am the Lord your God who brought you out of the land of Egypt, with the intention that you be slaves no longer; I have broken your chains and will make you walk with dignity.
Deuteronomy 8:3 LB	He did it to help you realize that food isn't everything, and that real life comes by obeying every command of God.
Psalms 37:5 LB	Commit everything you do to the Lord. Trust him to help you do it and he will.
Psalms 78:18, 19 AMPLIFIED	And they tempted God in their heart by asking food according to their *selfish* desire *and* appetite. Yes, they spoke against God; they said, Can God fur-

Old Testament

nish [the food for] a table in the wilderness?

Psalms 118:8
LB
It is better to trust the Lord than to put confidence in men.

Proverbs 3:5, 6
KJV
Trust in the Lord with all thine heart; and lean not unto thine own understanding. In all thy ways acknowledge him, and he shall direct thy paths.

Proverbs 13:3
AMPLIFIED
He who guards his mouth keeps his life, but he who opens wide his lips will come to ruin.

Proverbs 13:25
LB
The good man eats to live, while the evil man lives to eat.

Proverbs 21:23
LB
Keep your mouth closed and you'll stay out of trouble.

Proverbs 23:21
KJV
For the drunkard and the glutton shall come to poverty . . . .

Isaiah 41:10
LB
Fear not, for I am with you. Do not be dismayed. I am your God. I will strengthen you; I will help you; I will uphold you with my victorious right hand.

Isaiah 61:1
KJV
The Spirit of the Lord God is upon me; because the Lord hath anointed me to preach . . . liberty to the captives, and the opening of the prison to them that are bound . . . .

New Testament

Matthew 5:6
AMPLIFIED

Blessed *and* fortunate *and* happy *and* spiritually prosperous [that is, in that state in which the born-again child of God enjoys His favor and salvation] are those who hunger and thirst for righteousness (uprightness and right standing with God) for they shall be completely satisfied!

Matthew 6:21, 25, 31, 33
AMPLIFIED

For where your treasure is, there will your heart be also . . . . Therefore I tell you, stop being perpetually uneasy (anxious and worried) about your life, what you shall eat *or what you shall drink,* and about your body, what you shall put on. Is not life greater [in quality] than food, and the body [far above and more excellent] than clothing? . . . Therefore do not worry *and* be anxious, saying, What are we going to have to eat? or, What are we going to have to drink? or, What are we going to have to wear? . . . But seek for (aim at and strive after) first of all His kingdom, and His righteousness [His way of doing

New Testament

and being right], and then all these things taken together will be given you besides.

John 8:36
KJV

If the Son therefore shall make you free, ye shall be free indeed.

John 10:14
LB

"I am the Good Shepherd and know my own sheep, and they know me."

Romans 6:16
LB

Don't you realize that you can choose your own master? You can choose sin (with death) or else obedience (with acquittal). The one to whom you offer yourself—he will take you and be your master and you will be his slave.

Romans 8:1, 2
LB

So there is now no condemnation awaiting those who belong to Christ Jesus. For the power of the life-giving Spirit—and this power is mine through Christ Jesus—has freed me from the vicious circle of sin and death.

Romans 8:5
AMPLIFIED

For those who are according to the flesh *and* controlled by its unholy desires, set their minds on *and* pursue those things which gratify the flesh. But those who are according to the

New Testament

Romans 8:9–11
AMPLIFIED

Spirit *and* [controlled by the desires] of the Spirit, set their minds on *and* seek those things which gratify the (Holy) Spirit. But you are not living the life of the flesh, you are living the life of the Spirit, if the (Holy) Spirit of God [really] dwells within you—directs *and* controls you. But if any one does not possess the (Holy) Spirit of Christ, he is none of His—he does not belong to Christ [is not truly a child of God]. But if Christ lives in you, [then although your natural] body is dead by reason of sin *and* guilt, the spirit is alive because of [the] righteousness [that He imputes to you]. And if the Spirit of Him Who raised up Jesus from the dead dwells in you, [then] He Who raised up Christ *Jesus* from the dead will also restore to life your mortal (short-lived, perishable) bodies through His Spirit Who dwells in you.

Romans 12:1
KJV

I beseech you therefore, brethren, by the mercies of God, that ye present your bodies a living sacrifice, holy, acceptable unto

New Testament

God, which is your reasonable service.

Romans 13:14
AMPLIFIED

But clothe yourself with the Lord Jesus Christ, the Messiah, and make no provision for [indulging] the flesh—put a stop to thinking about the evil cravings of your physical nature—to [gratify its] desires (lusts).

Romans 14:17
KJV

For the kingdom of God is not meat and drink; but righteousness, and peace, and joy in the Holy Ghost.

1 Corinthians 3:16
PHILLIPS

Make no mistake: you are God's holy building. Don't you realize that you yourselves are the temple of God, and that God's Spirit lives in you?

1 Corinthians 6:19
AMPLIFIED

Do you not know that your body is the temple—the very sanctuary—of the Holy Spirit Who lives within you, Whom you have received [as a Gift] from God? You are not your own.

1 Corinthians 6:20
LB

For God has bought you with a great price. So use every part of your body to give glory back to God, because he owns it.

1 Corinthians 9:27
LB

Like an athlete I punish my body, treating it roughly, train-

Freedom from Fat

New Testament

ing it to do what it should, not what it wants to. Otherwise I fear that after enlisting others for the race, I myself might be declared unfit and ordered to stand aside.

1 Corinthians 10:13
LB

No temptation is irresistible. You can trust God to keep the temptation from becoming so strong that you can't stand up against it, for he has promised this and will do what he says. He will show you how to escape temptation's power so that you can bear up patiently against it.

1 Corinthians 15:57
LB

It is he who makes us victorious through Jesus Christ our Lord!

2 Corinthians 3:17
KJV

Where the Spirit of the Lord is, there is liberty.

2 Corinthians 7:1
LB

Having such great promises as these, dear friends, let us turn away from everything wrong, whether of body or spirit, and purify ourselves, living in the wholesome fear of God, giving ourselves to him alone.

2 Corinthians 10:3–5
AMPLIFIED

For though we walk [live] in the flesh, we are not carrying on our warfare according to the flesh *and* using mere human

New Testament

weapons. For the weapons of our warfare are not physical (weapons of flesh and blood), but they are mighty before God for the overthrow *and* destruction of strongholds, [Inasmuch as we] refute arguments *and* theories *and* reasonings and every proud *and* lofty thing that sets itself up against the (true) knowledge of God; and we lead every thought *and* purpose away captive into the obedience of Christ, the Messiah, the Anointed One.

2 Corinthians 12:9
LB

"No. But I am with you; [God said to me, Paul.] that is all you need. My power shows up best in weak people." Now I am glad to boast about how weak I am; I am glad to be a living demonstration of Christ's power, instead of showing off my own power and abilities.

Galatians 5:1
KJV

Stand fast therefore in the liberty wherewith Christ hath made us free, and be not entangled again with the yoke of bondage.

Galatians 5:16, 17
KJV

This I say then, Walk in the Spirit, and ye shall not fulfill the lust of the flesh. For the

New Testament

flesh lusteth against the Spirit, and the Spirit against the flesh: and these are contrary the one to the other: so that ye cannot do the things that ye would.

Philippians 2:13
LB

For God is at work within you, helping you want to obey him, and then helping you do what he wants.

Philippians 4:13
LB

For I can do everything God asks me to with the help of Christ who gives me the strength and power.

Colossians 3:1, 2
KJV

If ye then be risen with Christ, seek those things which are above, where Christ sitteth on the right hand of God. Set your affection on things above, not on things on the earth.

1 Thessalonians 2:12
LB

That your daily lives should not embarrass God, but bring joy to him who invited you into his kingdom to share his glory.

1 Thessalonians 5:23
LB

May the God of peace himself make you entirely pure and devoted to God; and may your spirit and soul and body be kept strong and blameless until that day when our Lord Jesus Christ comes back again.

New Testament

Hebrews 4;15, 16
LB

This High Priest of ours understands our weaknesses, since he had the same temptations we do, though he never once gave way to them and sinned. So let us come boldly to the very throne of God and stay there to receive his mercy and to find grace to help us in our times of need.

1 Peter 2:11
KJV

Dearly beloved, I beseech you as strangers and pilgrims, abstain from fleshly lusts, which war against the soul.

Bibliography

Dawson, Joy. *How to Hear God's Voice*. Truth Tapes, Box 1099, Sunland, CA. 91040.

———. *Some Reasons Why God Delays Answers*. Truth Tapes.

———. *The Ways God Speaks*. Truth Tapes.

Moe, Thelma. *Fruit of the Spirit*. Washington: Aglow Publications, 1974.

Thomas, Ann. *God's Answer to Overeating*. Washington: Aglow Publications, 1975.

Wallis, Arthur. *God's Chosen Fast*. Washington, Pennsylvania: Christian Literature Crusade, 1968.